FILMS OF THE
FRENCH
FOREIGN
LEGION

PHILIP LEIBFRIED

BearManor Media
Albany, Georgia

The Films of the French Foreign Legion
Copyright © 2011 Philip Leibfried. All rights reserved.

All rights reserved. No portion of this publication may be reproduced, stored, and/or copied electronically (except for academic use as a source), nor transmitted in any form or by any means without the prior written permission of the publisher and/or the author.

Published in the USA by:
BearManor Media
PO Box 1129
Duncan, OK 73534-1129
www.BearManorMedia.com

ISBN 1-59393-673-7
ISBN-13: 978-1-59393-673-0

Printed in the United States.

Design and Layout by Allan T. Duffin.

Table of Contents

Acknowledgements   vii

Introduction   ix

Chapter One: 1
Seminal Sands: Under Two Flags

Chapter Two: 17
Celebrated Sands: The Novels of P. C. Wren

Chapter Three: 37
Silent Sands: Cinema de Legion 1914–1928

Chapter Four: 49
Sound Sands: Cinema de Legion 1929–2000

Chapter Five: 67
Singing Sands: Legion Musicals

Chapter Six: 75
Shifting Sands: Films of the Post-World War II Legion

Chapter Seven: 85
Subtitled Sands: Foreign Foreign Legion Films

Chapter Eight: 113
Satiric Sands: Comedies and Cartoons

Chapter Nine: 131
Sundry Sands: The Legion on the Stage, Radio and Television

Chapter Ten: 149
Superfluous Sands: Marginal French Foreign Legion Films and Spanish Foreign Legion Films

Bibliography   159

Index   163

Acknowledgments

First and foremost of the contributors to this volume is my good friend Pierre Guinle of Brussels, Belgium, the world's greatest admirer of the bravest of the brave. His booklet on French Foreign Legion films, *Filmografia della Legione Straniera*, published in Italy in 1992, laid the groundwork for this book. He unselfishly kept me updated on all European productions about the Legion. Without his assistance and support, this project would still be in the works. *Merci, mon ami!*

In terms of amount of material supplied, the prize must go to Madeline Matz, formerly of the Library of Congress, who has been there for me on all my film history projects. To her former colleague, Alice L. Birney, Literary Manuscript Historian, many thanks for her help with the stage adaptations. Honorable mention goes to my friend John Cocchi, for the loan of many stills, as well as for his selflessness in gathering needed reviews and credits.

Special thanks to Ned Thanhouser of the Thanhouser Film Company for supplying me with a DVD of the 1912 Thanhouser version of *Under Two Flags*, one of the earliest films mentioned in this book, as well as background material for it. To Sr. P. Ernesto Roman of the Cineteca Nacional of Mexico, much gratitude for supplying information on Legion films made in Mexico. Many thanks to the mysterious and very gracious Señor CJM de H for his assistance with Spanish Foreign Legion films.

To my long-time friend, illustrator Gary Zaboly, I owe much gratitude for his sending needed material and for his enthusiasm for the project. Frank Thompson, another huge Legion fan, gets special thanks for support and for supplying many of the photos seen herein. His forthcoming *Legend of the French Foreign Legion* DVD includes everything about the force not covered in this book. Sincere thanks to Ted K. Hering for sending data on some obscure television shows.

To my good friend Teel James Glenn, stuntman and fight choreographer supreme, much gratitude for the loan of obscure material as well as your support. To Mark Johnson for acquisition of videos goes my sincere gratitude. Dick Baker rates many thanks for his fantastic aid with credits for *The Goon Show*. To Jack Shaheen I owe much gratitude for his assistance and support. Special thanks to Luigi Cazzinaga for his generous assistance with some of the Italian film synopses.

And, of course, my thanks to my regular lifetime crew of supporters: Ann Chase, Estella Johnson, Chei Mi Lane, Annette D'Agostino Lloyd, Jim Low, Ellen Lytle, Jane MacDonald, Jannine Corti Petska, George Rackus, Frances Whalen, Michael Whalen, Richard Whalen and Fred Yannantuono.

§

Introduction

Beneath the scorching North African sun, an adobe fort stands alone amid vast sand dunes, besieged by hordes of robed tribesmen. Inside, a skeleton garrison of men clad in blue jackets and white kepis fights bravely, ready to die to the last man. Urged on by a brutal sergeant, they give a good account of themselves until both water and ammunition run out. As the attackers get ready for a final assault, the piercing notes of a bugle cut through the burning air. A relief column has arrived! The defenders will live to fight another day.

This is the picture which most filmgoers think of whenever the French Foreign Legion is mentioned, along with long lines of legionnaires trudging wearily across expansive desert wastes. While most Hollywood films about the Legion recall similar scenes, the truth was far less romantic, and the setting frequently very different. During its one-hundred-eighty-year history, the Legion has seen action all over the world. In fact, its most glorious *passage d'arms* occurred in the small Mexican town of Camerone on April 30, 1863. There, a force of sixty-five legionnaires held off some two thousand Mexican infantry and cavalry for nine hours from a farmhouse. The commanding officer, Captain Jean Danjou, who had lost his left arm at Sebastopol during the Crimean War and wore a wooden prosthesis, demanded an oath to fight to the death from his remaining troops. Shortly thereafter he was killed, but his men continued to fight. As the Mexicans launched their final attack, they were met by a bayonet charge from the five remaining able-bodied legionnaires. Two of them were killed, the others taken prisoner. When it was over, there was one officer and twenty-two wounded legionnaires left alive. The Mexicans counted three hundred casualties. Danjou's wooden hand was recovered and is displayed proudly every year on April 30 in a parade at the Foreign Legion museum in Aubagne.

Created by an order of King Louis Philippe of France in 1831, the *legion etrangers* originally served as a means of ridding France of thousands of political refugees who had sought asylum there after revolutions in their own countries in Southern and Eastern Europe. This law specifically stated that the enlistees were to serve only outside France, thus solving the problem of supporting hordes of non-citizens. One of the incentives used to attract those fugitives was the promise of French citizenship once their military service had ended. Among the stipulations of the royal order was that applicants be between the ages of eighteen and forty and not less than five feet in height.

The idea of hiring foreign troops was nothing new. Prior to this particular piece of legislation such troops saw action within the borders of whatever nation had hired them.

The Legion's beginning was less than sterling in military terms. Legionnaires did more road and fort building than fighting, and the desertion rate was high. It was only after years of unsuccessful campaigns that it began to earn its current reputation as arguably the most elite fighting force ever formed and, later, the most romanticized. Once established, the Legion became involved wherever France did, including both world wars. In the late nineteenth century, the first books and plays about the Foreign Legion began appearing, leading to its being noticed by a wider audience. The second decade of the twentieth century saw the first motion pictures made about the corps, further disseminating its already considerable fame.

It was the immense popularity of a novel published in 1924 by a former legionnaire that set the groundwork for most Hollywood films about the French Foreign Legion. First filmed in 1926, Percival Christopher Wren's *Beau Geste* has been remade only three times as a theatrical feature, but its leading characters, including an ogre of a sergeant, have influenced generations of filmmakers and filmgoers. An immediate bestseller, the quintessential Foreign Legion novel remains the most renowned depiction of Legion life, despite numerous personal memoirs written by former legionnaires over the years.

There are a number of elements of the French Foreign Legion that account for its attraction to so many: its superiority as a fighting force, the exotic setting of North Africa with its numerous tribes and cultures (though the Legion has fought all over the globe, the films are usually set in either Algeria or Morocco); the uniqueness of the uniforms with their kerchief-backed white kepis and long blue jackets (here is another popular inaccuracy; that uniform was in use only during the early twentieth century); and, the mystery surrounding the men who make up the Legion. Mostly dregs of society and mercenaries from many lands, some legionnaires have been of the nobility and high society who changed their names upon entering the Legion. For the musically inclined, there is also the most buoyant march this side of Sousa, "Marche de la Legion Etragére". This fascination has led to the French Foreign Legion's being represented in every area of the media--film, stage plays, radio and television--for over a century.

The following pages give as near a complete listing of such depictions as possible through 2007. An interesting side note regarding the films--in both the silent and sound eras, many leading actors appeared in Foreign Legion films, but these motion pictures have been given short shrift in biographies and autobiographies of those performers. Apparently, movies about the Foreign Legion are not as highly regarded as the outfit itself.

§

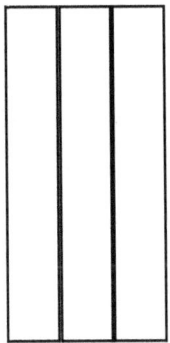

CHAPTER ONE
Seminal Sands: Under Two Flags

The book considered to be the first novel about the French Foreign Legion is not about the Legion at all, but the *Chasseurs d'Afrique*, the light cavalry branch of the French Army. However, it has often been misrepresented as a work about the Foreign Legion, including in the sole sound film adaptation, so it merits an in-depth mention here.

That such a work should be written by a woman may appear odd to some. It is not so strange, however, when one considers who that woman was. Born Maria Louise de la Ramée, on New Year's Day, 1839, on the outskirts of Bury St. Edmunds in Great Britain, she wrote under the pen name of "Ouida" (a childish pronunciation of "Louise"). Her mother was British and her father French; it was the latter who instilled in her a love of literature. He also told her many fanciful stories in her early years, when she was most impressionable. She lived in an idealistically romantic world, believing every man she met loved her deeply, as she did them. Her literary idol was Lord Byron, the epitome of Romanticism. She had her first story published in *Bentley's Miscellany*, a popular magazine of the day, when she was only twenty, and soon her work began appearing on a regular basis.

Part of her success was due to timing; in mid-Victorian England, reading was one of the few pastimes considered respectable, so it was indulged in fervently by all who were literate. There was also a dearth of the type of material which she wrote. Her flamboyant style and bold imagination allowed the middle and lower classes to look into the lives of the secretive upper class. Though riddled with inaccuracies (called "Ouidaisms" by the upper class), her style was such as to make her writings seem accurate. From all accounts, she herself was terribly affected and arrogant, always rude to her guests, as she thought more of the lower orders than of humans. Were she alive today, she would undoubtedly be both a staunch feminist and animal rights activist. She died penniless on January 25, 1908, and was buried in Italy. *Under Two Flags*, published in three volumes in December 1867, remains the best known of her forty-seven novels. It had initially been published that summer in a British military magazine entitled *New London*. A dramatization of the work was performed at the Lyceum Theatre in London on March 10, 1908 (see Chapter 9), to raise money for a memorial fund for the author.

Under Two Flags is a romantic work in more than one sense. A tale of love, involving a triangle of two women and one man, it is also an adventure story set in the remote Sahara Desert in the French colony of Algeria. Bert Cecil, scion of a noble British family, flees to Africa and joins the *Chasseurs d'Afrique* in order to save his ne'er-do-well younger brother's good name. There he becomes the object of affection of a half-breed camp-follower named Cigarette, who twice saves his life after encounters with Bedouins. He, however, falls in love with an English noblewoman. Condemned to death before a firing squad for striking an officer, Cecil is spared when Cigarette, carrying a pardon, steps between him and the riflemen. She dies in his arms, and Cecil eventually returns to England when his younger brother confesses to his earlier crimes.

Besides being a bestseller, *Under Two Flags* became the inspiration for two of the first four motion pictures to deal with the Legion almost a half-century later. The first two versions were both released in July of 1912, and each was two reels in length. Thanhouser's was released on July 7, with an ad in *The Moving Picture World* that read: "Ouida's greatest story issued as a sterling 'Thanhouser Classic' with an all-star cast--all the Thanhouser favorites. Filmed precisely the way Ouida wrote it--every situation thrills and startles." The only surviving print has a number of frames missing, totaling about four minutes, including the last half of Cigarette's heroic ride and her sacrifice; she suddenly appears limp in Cecil's arms. The direction is interesting, utilizing several aerial shots and some stately homes in Westchester County in New York, where the Thanhouser studio was located. It was the rule rather than the exception in those far-off days to produce accurate interpretations of literary works, since they were being made for members of the middle-class, who were being attracted to films by just such productions.

The second version was produced by Gem, a company about which little is known except that it was one of Universal's prestige labels, which only existed from June 1912 to October 1913. It was released one reel at a time, a week apart, on July 9 and 16, respectively. *The Moving Picture World* for July 13 thought highly of it, noting the paucity of intertitles.

It was three years before the next adaptation appeared, this time from Biograph, in a three-reel production. Reviewed by Lynde Denig in *The Moving Picture World* for July 3, 1915, this production was lauded as "Finely presented at all times..." and "The sandstorm in the desert is in itself enough to distinguish the production as something out of the ordinary."

The following year saw the release of yet a fourth interpretation, from Fox, starring the quintessential vamp, Theda Bara (1885-1955), as Cigarette, "the darling of the Legion." The heat in this milieu (though the picture was filmed at Montauk Point, Long Island) must have affected Bara's normal histrionics, for both *Variety* and *Motography* praised her acting, and gave the production an excellent review. The former stated "The picture is cleverly constructed and the views are as good as the best," while the latter had this to say: "...handled by J. Gordon Edwards in a very capable manner. Desert scenes are very realistic, but a sandstorm ... falls short of its mark." Well, nobody's perfect.

Theda Bara and Fox studio executives

Under Two Flags was Theda Bara's fifteenth film, her sixth for 1916 in which she appeared in no fewer than nine pictures, tying 1915 as her most prolific year. Four years and twenty-one pictures later, her brief but spectacular career was over, as such overexposure proved to be her downfall. She made an unsuccessful stab at the stage, followed by two film appearances in the twenties, and then vanished from show business for good. She spent the rest of her life happily married to director Charles Brabin (1883-1957). An added twist to her disappearance occurred in the late thirties, when a fire at a Fox storeroom destroyed the negatives of all but her first film, *Sic transit gloria*.

The most lavish of the five silent adaptations of *Under Two Flags* was produced by Universal in 1922. This one also utilized the proper milieu of the *Chasseurs d'Afrique*. Starring their top female lead of the time, Priscilla Dean (1896-1988), as Cigarette, the film was directed by Tod Browning (1882-1962), who was to become noted for his collaborations with star character actor Lon Chaney on several memorable pictures. Browning also co-authored the screenplay for this eight-reel feature, which, though billed as "The Picture Magnificent" by the studio, failed to overly impress the critic for *The New York Times*, who wrote: "...the picture seemed to drag in spots, despite Priscilla Dean's efforts." But he did like the sandstorm sequence. (As well he should have; while filming that sequence in Oxnard, a real storm occurred which buried the wind machines Browning had brought up from Hollywood. Fortunately, the cameraman had the presence of mind to capture nature's response to the presumptive filmmakers by keeping his camera rolling.)

Under Two Flags (Universal, 1922) magazine ad

The lone sound interpretation of Ouida's novel flashed across the nation's theater screens in 1936, in a major production by Twentieth Century-Fox. Cigarette was portrayed by Claudette Colbert (1905-1996), who replaced French actress Simone Simon (1911-2004). Ronald Colman (1891-1958) returned to the scene of his greatest silent film triumph of a decade earlier, *Beau Geste* (see Chapter 2), playing Sgt. Victor in this version of Ouida's romance. This production was slated to be directed by Tod Browning for Universal, but they sold the rights to Fox. It was also incorrectly set in the Foreign Legion; in fact, the film opens with a copy of the book, the cover of which contains the subtitle "A Story of the French Foreign Legion," in order to justify the difference. This time the main accent was placed on Colman's character rather than on the half-breed Cigarette. The popular actor, regarded as the quintessential British gentleman, was in the midst of his finest period, having just appeared in *A Tale of Two Cities* (1935) and with *Lost Horizon* and *The Prisoner of Zenda* looming one year ahead. He had also been voted "the handsomest man in Hollywood" in 1935 by a poll taken among fifty-one actresses.

Ouida's mid-nineteenth-century story was updated to the early twentieth century in this adaptation, and there are several other differences as well. Sergeant Victor's true name here is Rafe Brett; the commander of the post, played by Victor McLaglen (1886-1959), is shown as a rival for Cigarette's affections; the beginning of the novel is jettisoned, with all the action taking place in North Africa; and Cigarette dies as she leads a company of *chasseurs* to rescue Victor from a desert chieftain, rather than from a firing squad.

It was all directed in the grand manner in just over eight weeks by Frank Lloyd (1888-1960), who had just helmed the highly successful *Mutiny on the Bounty* (1935) for M-G-M, winning the Best Picture Academy Award in the process. The entire cast performs with enthusiasm, and the photography is stunning, especially the scenes shot in the Arizona desert outside Yuma, with sweeping vistas of towering sand dunes beneath cloud-studded skies. Rousing battle scenes add much excitement to this production, but unfortunately occur only in the second half of the film. This fact notwithstanding, *Under Two Flags* was still a box-office smash, opening at Radio City Music Hall in New York to fine reviews.

An interesting note is the role played by renowned character actor John Carradine (1906-1988), that of a legionnaire named "Cafard." In Legion parlance, "Le Cafard" refers to the madness of *ennui* suffered by many legionnaires; its literal translation is "the cockroach," meaning that boredom eats away at one's brain like that insect might. Unfortunately, all of Carradine's footage was excised before the film's release.

Written in florid style, this once-popular novel has likely seen its final filmization, for the present world has little use for such sentiment as its author expressed.

Filmography

UNDER TWO FLAGS

Thanhouser. Released July 7, 1912. 2 reels. Director: Lucius Henderson. Scenario: Theodore Marston, based on the novel by Ouida (Marie Louise de la Ramée). Cast: Katherine Horn, Florence La Badie, William Garwood, Alphonse Ethier, William Russell, Harry Benham, William Bowman.

The Morning Telegraph, July 14, 1912: "It has been splendidly staged by the Thanhouser Company and is acted in a thoroughly artistic manner throughout....last half is full of dramatic action. The desert scenes are pictured with a marvelous naturalness....the sand storm is one of the finest effects recently photographed...."

The Moving Picture World, July 20, 1912: "The second reel...is better than the first. There is a sandstorm in the desert...which is effective. The work of the whole company is of the best and the same may be said of the directing."

New York Dramatic Mirror, July 17, 1912: "...many interesting scenes and a good deal of passable acting."

Synopsis: Bertie Cecil, heir and eldest son of an English viscount, has fled from his regiment to shield his brother, who has committed forgery. He takes the blame upon himself, and the search is soon dropped, for it is believed that he has been killed in a train wreck. In fact, he has reached Algeria, where he has enlisted in the French Foreign Legion. There, he wins fame as a gallant soldier, but he fails to garner a promotion because his colonel, for personal reasons, hates him; after twelve years in France's service, he has only attained the rank of corporal, despite his record. A beautiful young *vivandier* named Cigarette meets Cecil and falls in love with him. Cigarette has been with the army all her young life, and her bravery and patriotism has won all hearts. She saves the detachment to which Cecil is assigned from destruction by hostile Arabs, and to recompense her, it is decreed that she be made a member of the Legion of Honor. When the presentation is made by a marshal of France, a number of English people, guests of the colonel, witness it. Cigarette, who watches Cecil jealously, sees that he recognizes the strangers, although they do not notice him. A day or so later, one Englishwoman and the party surprise Cecil, who is kissing a tiny purse. This woman is the sister of Cecil's dearest friend, Lord Rockingham, and years before, when she was a young girl, she had given it to Cecil with all her pocket money, because she was sorry when he had lost a horse race. Refusing the money, he had made her very happy by asking for the purse. This link of the love of long ago betrays Bertie's secret, and he confesses his identity, but makes the woman promise not to tell anyone. They meet frequently, however, and one evening they are surprised by the colonel. He makes a sneering remark and Cecil knocks him down. For this serious offense Cecil is court-martialed and sentenced to death. Cigarette, who by this time has realized that her hero is meant not for her, decides to save him. By a wonderful ride she reaches the headquarters of the marshal, sent in her Legion of Honor insignia as a credential, and by her argument wins a pardon for the brave soldier. She starts back again in a race against death. On the way she encounters a sandstorm, but fights her way through it. Her horse exhausted, she makes her way to a camp of Arabs, knowing that they seek her life. She tells them that she will consent to be their prisoner, on condition that they speedily forward the pardon in time to save a brave soldier unjustly condemned. The Arabs, won by her heroism, set her at liberty, give her a fresh horse, and she reaches the camp just as the firing squad is raising their muskets. Rushing in front of the prisoner, she waves the pardon in the air, receiving in her own body the bullets that are fired at Cecil. She lives long enough to tell him that she knows he will be happy with the English girl - and then she dies. Cecil, his honor restored by the tardy confession of his weak brother, returns to England to claim the fortune and title that are his, his father having died. And although his married life is happy, he often thinks of the girl who gave her life for him.

UNDER TWO FLAGS

Gem. Released July 9 and 16, 1912. 2 reels. Director: George Nicholls. Based on the novel by Ouida (Marie Louise de la Ramée). Cast: Vivian Preston, Herschel Mayall, Charles Perley, H. R. Nathanson.

The Moving Picture World, July 13, 1912: "This picture...is singularly independent of sub-titles. In fact, there were none at all in the print seen by the reviewer, and the story told itself well enough. However, there must be sub-titles where there are lapses of time, and such are the only ones needed in the cinematographic reproduction of 'Under Two Flags.' A sandstorm also is cleverly done by the aid of photographic manipulation. The scenes portraying soldiery and clashes of arms are especially well handled and full of rapid action."

Seminal Sands: Under Two Flags

Synopsis: Bertie Cecil is a member of England's nobility and of the National Guardsmen. He finds diversion in innocent flirtations with married women. Lady Guinevere likes him and determines to keep the romance from her husband's observation. Bertie's brother, Berkeley, loses heavily at gambling and asks Bertie for financial assistance. Bertie sadly explains that he cannot even meet his own debts. That night Lady Guinevere visits Cecil. Berkeley goes to a money lender and offers him a note for sufficient funds to cover the deficit and signs his brother's name and has it endorsed by a friend, Lord Rockingham. Not long after, the last of Bertie's fortune is wiped out. Rockingham's eight-year-old sister comes to him and offers some gold. Bertie says he cannot accept it, explaining that she will know the reason when she becomes a woman. He asks for the little enamel box in which she brought the gold as a memento and receives it just as he is summoned to Rockingham's quarters. There, he finds Rockingham and the money lender with the forged note. The nobleman pleads with him to deny the charge and explain where he was the night the note was executed. By speaking, he compromises a woman; by remaining silent, it must be accepted as an admission of guilt. He remains silent. When the money lender tries to put handcuffs on him, he escapes and goes to Africa where he enlists with the French military. Ten years later, Bertie is still in the French service and being loved by Cigarette, the daughter of the army. The memory of his earlier life still lingers, however. Among some British visitors to the barracks is a very young and beautiful woman. They become acquainted and the woman develops an interest in Bertie. Cecil is wounded in a battle and Cigarette drags him to a shack where she nurses him. In his delirium Bertie calls the name of the Englishwoman. Choking back sobs, Cigarette leaves him so that he will not know of her love for him. One day the Englishwoman sees the enamel box, now rusty and battered. When she asks Cecil where he had obtained it, he tells her the story and she reveals herself as Rockingham's sister. She tells Bertie that her brother is with her and begs him to stay and meet him. Bertie asks her not to reveal his presence and leaves. Once on a street in Algiers, Bertie encounters his brother, who greets him with a vague, trembling fear. Bertie tells him to return to England with his title and honor. Bertie visits the Englishwoman one night, and is spotted by his colonel leaving her house. In a jealous rage, the colonel asks Bertie what he was doing there. He then insinuates that the woman was cold to her equals, but carried on intrigues with the blackguards of the camp. Before he realizes what he has done, Bertie strikes the colonel. Bertie is court-martialed, found guilty, and sentenced to be shot on the morrow. Cigarette hears of this and runs up a street where she meets Berkeley. She tells him all that has transpired and he confesses his crime. She has him write a confession and runs to the marshal's tent with the paper. She is handed a reprieve and rides to the French fort. Arriving at the scene of execution just as the command to fire is given, she shouts, "Stop! In the name of France!" and hurls herself in front of Cecil, taking the bullets meant for him. Bertie kisses her; she smiles fleetingly and dies. Back home in England, Cecil and Guinivere both think of the human cost of their happiness.

UNDER TWO FLAGS

Biograph. Released July 17, 1915. 3 reels. Director: Travers Vale. Scenario: Paul M. Potter, based on the novel by Ouida (Marie Louise de la Ramée). Cast: Louise Vale, Franklin Ritchie, Herbert Barrington, Jack Drumier, Helen Bray, Alan Hale, Charles H. Mailes, Kenneth Davenport.

The Moving Picture World, July 3, 1915: "...remarkable for the beauty of its settings, for the wealth of atmosphere attained and for artistic detail. Finely presented at all times, the dramatic value of the picture increases during the second and third reels..."

Synopsis: Bertie Cecil of the Guards loves but two things--his horse, Forest King, and his young brother, Berkeley. He has an affair with Lady Guenevere, but does not love her. At the height of his career, fate deals him a cruel blow through all three of these affections at once. His brother forges his name to a note, with that of his friend, Lord Rockingham, as endorser. The money lender settles an old score by "painting" his horse before a great race on which his fortunes are staked, and Forest King is beaten. Through an indiscretion, Lady Guenevere's honor is compromised. The note falling due, Bertie shields his brother by owning to the forgery, and flees the country. Rake, his soldier valet, goes with him. Their train is wrecked they are presumed dead, but they escape, go to Africa, and join the French *chasseurs*, who are fighting the Arabs. Here, Bertie meets Cigarette, a strange girl, "the daughter of the regiment." She falls in love with him. He incurs the enmity of his chief, the Black Hawk, by interfering when the officer insults the wife of the Arab chieftain, and for striking his officer he is sentenced to be shot. Cigarette rides through the night with a reprieve; arriving too late, she flings herself upon Bertie as a shield as the riflemen fire. His honor satisfied, Bertie returns home.

UNDER TWO FLAGS

Fox. Released July 31, 1916. 6 reels. Director: J. Gordon Edwards. Scenario: George Hall, based on the novel by Ouida (Marie Louise de la Ramée). Camera: Philip E. Rosen. Cast: Theda Bara, Herbert Heyes, Stuart Holmes, Claire Whitney, Stanhope Wheatcroft, Joseph Crehan, Charles Craig, Violet de Biccari. Re-released January 1919.

Variety, August 4, 1916: "...a corking good program feature...with a fine line of action from beginning to end...cleverly constructed and the views are as good as the best."

Motography, August 12, 1916: "The story gives Theda Bara ample opportunity to bear witness to the fact that her powers do not all lie in the direction of the vampire role. We get an entirely new view of this star...one which is illumined by sparkling gems of acting....The production was handled by J. Gordon Edwards in a very capable manner. Desert scenes are very realistic, but a sand storm...falls short of its mark."

Synopsis: Bertie Cecil, the eldest son of the Viscount Royalieu, takes upon himself the blame for his dissolute younger brother's crime and flees the country. He arrives in Algeria under an assumed name and joins the French army as a private. Due to aid which he renders the wife of an Arabian Emir, who has been abducted by the colonel in charge of the barracks, the Marquis de Chateauroye, he incurs the latter's lasting hatred. Bertie unconsciously wins the admiration and love of Cigarette, "the daughter of the regiment." In the course of time Venetia, Cecil's lover from childhood, and Berkeley, his brother, arrive at the French barracks as members of a distinguished English touring party. Bertie's intimacy with Venetia arouses Cigarette's jealousy and she tries to kill this intruder, an attempt which conscience overcomes. Finally, when Chateauroye insults Venetia, the long pent-up animosity of both men bursts forth and they engage in a fierce struggle. As a result, Bertie is sentenced to be shot for attacking his superior. Venetia, being a friend of the marshal of France, explains the situation to him through a letter which Cigarette carries to him on her swift horse. Cigarette obtains a reprieve from the marshal, but is delayed by Arabs on her return. She arrives at the barracks just as the firing squad is taking aim at Bertie and she dashes in front of them, only to receive the volley of bullets intended for him. The story closes with Venetia and Bertie together and the resolution of the difficulty caused by Berkeley.

UNDER TWO FLAGS

Universal-Jewel. Released September 24, 1922. 8 reels. Director: Tod Browning. Scenario: Edward T. Lowe, Jr. and Elliot Clawson, based on the novel by Ouida (Marie Louise de la Ramée) and the stage play by Paul Potter. Adaptation: Tod Browning and Edward T. Lowe, Jr. Photography: William Fildew. Editor: Errol Taggart. Art Director: E.E. Sheeley. Assistant Director: Leo McCarey. Titles: Gardner Bradford. Cast: Priscilla Dean, James Kirkwood, Stuart Holmes, Ethel Grey Terry, John Davidson, Robert Mack, Burton Law, Albert Pollet, W.H. Bainbridge, Fred Craven, the Oriental Ballet.

Moving Picture World, October 7, 1922: "Director Tod Browning has made an excellent production. ... Priscilla Dean...gives a fine portrayal.... The settings are spectacular and effective....."

Variety, September 29, 1922: "...is a world-beater for action and Priscilla Dean is wonderful in the role. Tod Browning did himself proud in the matter of direction...his action stuff with the battle in the desert stronghold, the ride to the rescue are all well handled."

Under Two Flags (Universal, 1922) Priscilla Dean and James Kirkwood

Synopsis: A mysterious figure appears at a café which is the meeting place of a French regiment stationed in Algiers. He approaches a corporal and asks to enlist. When he declines to give information regarding himself, other than his name is Victor, he is refused. He offers to play dice to see if he joins the French or their enemies, the Arabs. The corporal again refuses. Standing nearby is Cigarette, half-French, half-Arab, a child of the desert and "the daughter of the regiment." She leaps forward and agrees to play dice with Victor. He accepts her challenge and throws the dice. He loses and promises to report in the morning. Cigarette invites him to share a glass of champagne with her. Victor leaves without a word. It is the first time in her life that a man has failed to appreciate her charms and she vows vengeance. Years pass and Cigarette falls in love with the handsome Victor, who still repulses all her advances. His feats have won him fame and glory, but he is still a man of mystery. In the interim the Sheik Ben Ali Hammed has made overtures for a peace pact with Marquis deChateauroy, the commandant. The marquis has fallen into the trap and accepted. With his enemies lulled into a false sense of security, the sheik plans a desert uprising which will sweep the French from the desert forever. At this point a powerful English noblewoman, the Princess Corona, visits Algiers. During a visit to the French barracks, she is struck by some hand-carved work of Victor's and offers to buy it. He refuses to sell, but expresses a desire to make a present of it to the princess; she declines. The marquis is indignant at Victor, and becomes spiteful when he sees the politeness with which the common soldier has impressed the princess. He plans to arouse the trooper's wrath so far that he will forget himself and lay himself open to a court-martial. Cigarette senses his plan and warns Victor to be careful. That night Victor is summoned to the commandant's office. He maintains his reserve and leaves without letting the commandant get the better of him. The sheik, sensing how things are going, sees a chance to win Victor to his side and arranges to have him kidnapped on his way back to the barracks. Cigarette foils the plot and saves Victor's life. He is taken to his quarters where a fever sets in. During his delirium he divulges that he is of noble English birth and has fled the country assuming the guilt of a crime to save his brother. He also reveals that the princess is his one and only love from his days in England. Furious, Cigarette goes to the princess determined to kill her. The Englishwoman's bravery causes Cigarette to make a grudging admission that she can understand why Victor loves her. She then reveals Victor's true identity to the princess and enlists her sympathy. Meanwhile, the sheik is almost ready to strike. He tries to persuade Cigarette to go with him to the desert and become queen of his harem. She spurns his advances, but a short time later, having heard hints that he is plotting to attack with his desert hordes, returns and accepts his proposition. The sheik, just before leaving, decides to get Victor out of the way and hatches up a false charge of treason which he presents to the marquis. At the palace Cigarette learns of the plot to seize Algiers and annihilate the French. She kills the sheik, escapes, and after a wild desert chase arrives at the general's house. She has also learned of the plot against Victor, how it was framed, and that he is under sentence of death. Obtaining a parole for the man she loves, and with the French troops ready to meet the desert hordes, she rides like mad into Algiers. She arrives just in time to receive the bullets intended for Victor and dies in his arms, as the last of the Arabs are driven from the gates of the city.

Under Two Flags (Universal, 1922) **Priscilla Dean and John Davidson**

UNDER TWO FLAGS

Twentieth Century-Fox. Released April 30, 1936. 110mins. Director: Frank Lloyd. Producer: Darryl F. Zanuck. Screenplay: W.P. Lipscomb and Walter Ferris, from the novel by Ouida (Marie Louise de la Ramée). Settings: Thomas Little. Cinematographer: Ernest Palmer. Assistant Directors: Al Schaumer, A.F. Erickson. Musical Score: Louis Silvers. Director of Battle Sequences: Otto Brower. Battle Photography: Sidney Wagner. Special Effects: Edwin Hammeras, Fred Sersen. Technical Advisors: Otto Steiger, Douglas Baxter, Jamiel Hasson. Ballistics Expert: Louis Witte. Associate Producer: Raymond Griffith. Film Editor: Ralph Dietrich. Costumes: Gwen Wakeling. Unit Manager: Ben Silvey. Art Director: William Darling. Asst. Art Director: Eldo Chrysler. Sound: Joseph Aiken, Roger Heman. Makeup: Marie Brasselle, Tony Carnagle, Dick Narr. Set Dresser: Al Orenbach. Cast: Ronald Colman, Claudette Colbert, Victor McLaglen, Rosalind Russell, Gregory Ratoff, Nigel Bruce, C. Henry Gordon, Herbert Mundin, John Carradine, Lumsden Hare, J. Edward Bromberg, Onslow Stevens, Fritz Leiber, Thomas Beck, William Ricciardi, Frank Reicher, Francis McDonald, Harry Semels, Nicholas Soussanin, Douglas Gerrard, Frank Lackteen, Tor Johnson, Marc Lawrence, Gwendolen Logan, Jamiel Hasson, Hans von Morhart, Ronald J. Pennick, Rolfe Sedan, Eugene Borden, Harry Worth, Tony Merl, Alex Palasthy, Gaston Glass, Rosita Harlan, Fred Malatesta, Hector Sarno, Jean De Briac, George Jackson, Tony Merlo, George Ducount, William McCormick, Dave Dunbar, Al Thompson, Andre Cuyas, Juan Duval, Jack Wagner, Ray Jones, Stubby Kruger, Ralph Banks, Harry Dean, Joe Sawoya, Jack Kenny, Coit Albertson, Mason Litson, Chauncey Pyle, Gino Corrado, Carl De Loro, John George, Earl Hap Hogan, B. Martinez, Joe Dominguez, Charles Drubin, Steve Clemente, Karma Faris, Jacques Vanair, Rex Richards, George Sowards.

New York Times, May 1, 1936: "Twentieth Century-Fox has not stinted on its production...it manages, under Frank Lloyd's deft direction, to hold our interest during the quieter interludes when the Legion is not defending the Tricolor against the scourging forays of Sidi-Ben-Youssiff...."

Synopsis: In southern Algeria at the turn of the nineteenth century, a French-Algerian café hostess named Cigarette, the object of the affections of Major Doyle, flirts with Cpl. Victor, who at 18 saved his convoy from an attack by the rebel chieftain Sidi-Ben Youssiff. Victor ignores her. After Victor is promoted to sergeant, he sees Cigarette try to swindle a British officer in a horse deal and wagers a bottle of wine to a kiss that he can beat Cigarette in a race. After he wins, Victor further antagonizes Cigarette by offering his horse for her to kiss. When she rides off into the desert, he follows. They kiss and she confesses her love for him. Victor meets Lady Venetia Cunningham, the niece of the British commissioner, and after showing her the Arab village, invites her to a nearby oasis late at night. She refuses at first, but goes later and they spend the night together while Cigarette waits all night. War is declared after chieftain Ben Hamidou, a friend of the British, is murdered by followers of Sidi-Ben Youssiff. Before the troops depart, Victor learns that Lady Venetia is the niece of the visiting Lord Seraph. Worried that Seraph will recognize the little horse that Victor gave to the lady, he sneaks into Venetia's room to retrieve it. They confess their love for each other, and Victor tells the lady that he will be imprisoned if he returns to England. Meanwhile, Doyle, who is now a major, discovers that Cigarette loves Victor. After the battalion leaves, Lord Seraph finds the little horse and tells Lady Venetia that it was once given to him by

Rafe Brett, a popular officer who disappeared after taking the blame for a crime committed by his younger brother, and who has since been completely cleared. Lady Venetia confronts Cigarette and discovers that Doyle has been sending Victor on very dangerous missions, hoping that he will be killed. She asks Cigarette to save Victor. She refuses, knowing of his love for Venetia. Meanwhile, Doyle begins to feel remorse for his treatment of Victor and orders his battalion to rescue Victor and his men. During a battle, Doyle is shot in the shoulder. Later, when the battalion is surrounded, Victor tells Doyle that he is not in love with Cigarette. Victor then meets with Sidi-Ben Youssiff to stall for time as Cigarette leads some French reinforcements. During the battle she is shot and dies in Victor's arms. He first tells her that he will always remember that day in the desert and kisses her. The revolt is prevented and Cigarette receives a military funeral.

Under Two Flags (20th Century-Fox, 1936) Rosalind Russell and Claudette Colbert

While preparing this production, Twentieth Century-Fox was advised by its legal department to avoid using material from any of the previous stage dramatizations (see Chapter 9). At that time, 1935, the motion picture rights to the play were owned by Universal. Before their merger with Twentieth Century Pictures, Fox purchased the rights from Universal for $25,000 in May 1935.

French actress Simone Simon was signed to make her American film debut as Cigarette. She was fired just two weeks after filming began at the request of director Lloyd, who became fed up with her temperamental attitude. Her footage was scrapped and Claudette Colbert replaced her. The studio released press notices to the effect that Miss Simon was bowing out due to illness.

Location shooting was done at the California-Arizona desert site near where the 1926 *Beau Geste* had been filmed. The battle scenes utilized the services of local cowpunchers, Yuma Indians and Hollywood extras. A ten-acre desert village was built on the studio's Westwood lot. The picture had a budget of $1,250,000 and took about four months to produce, from December 1935 to March 1936.

In one scene, Colman was to have a knife thrown at him by Cigarette; the blade was supposed to hit a post near him. A Yacqui knife-thrower, who had not missed his mark in twenty years, was hired to perform the stunt. Due to the man's expertise, Colman did not use a double. The knife hit him sideways in the chest, causing a large bruise. The Yacqui claimed that he was distracted. All the leading players were insured for $5,000 against camel bites.

Frank Lloyd was so unhappy with studio head Darryl F. Zanuck's (1902-1979) cutting of his film that he vowed never to work for Twentieth Century-Fox again, and never did.

§

Under Two Flags (Twentieth Century-Fox, 1936) Poster

CHAPTER TWO
Celebrated Sands:
The Novels of P.C. Wren

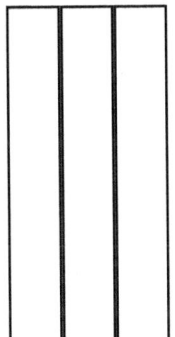

Among the top bestselling books of 1924 was a novel about the French Foreign Legion by a former member of that famed fighting corps, an Englishman by the name of Percival Christopher Wren (1885-1941). Little else is known of Wren except that he was a collateral descendant of renowned 17th- century architect Sir Christopher Wren and that he was an Oxford graduate. He married in London in 1917, where he lived for the rest of his life, which he spent in writing. There is no biography of the author to date.

The story of the unshakable bond among three brothers, *Beau Geste* contains action, adventure, mystery, and a character by the name of Sgt. LeJaune, who became a symbol of cruelty as great as Simon Legree. Despite the realism of the harsh Legion regimen depicted in this book, enlistments rose considerably after its publication. The book went through sixty-one editions by October 1937; the first paperback version was published by Pocket Books in 1940. One of many readers of the work was top Hollywood director Herbert Brenon (1880-1958), who immediately pitched the idea of filming it to Adolph Zukor, head of Paramount Pictures. Brenon was given the go-ahead and allowed a budget of $900,000, a very tidy sum in 1926. Originally, the exteriors were to be filmed on location in the French colony of Algeria, but the ongoing Riff War there made that an impossibility. Needing an alternative location resembling the North African region, the company selected the desert areas east of Burlingame, California, and southwest of Yuma, Arizona, near the Mexican border. Location shooting began in March of 1926 and wrapped in June.

The logistics of creating this film masterpiece are rather impressive. Besides the transport needed for the 2,000 or so players, it took seventeen trains to carry the necessary gear, livestock, and supplies from Los Angeles to Yuma before transferring to plank roads which ran into the desert filming sites. Ronald Colman's career, which had been steadily building, hit a new pinnacle with his portrayal of Beau Geste. Realizing his popularity, his employer, Samuel Goldwyn, never again lent him to another studio while Colman was under contract to him.

Beau Geste (Paramount, 1926) Production shot at Fort Zinderneuf

Beau Geste (Paramount, 1926) Ralph Forbes, Ronald Colman, Neil Hamilton

A humorous sidelight to the filming was recalled by actor Neil Hamilton (1899-1984), who played Digby Geste. When setting up the shot wherein 1,500 Arab horsemen attack the dwindling garrison at Fort Zinderneuf, director Brenon promised an extra ten dollars to any man who would make a good fall off his horse. With the cameras rolling, the "Arabs" rode full tilt towards the fort, which contained a mere twenty-two defenders. The latter fired on cue, and all 1,500 of the enemy fell off their mounts, ruining the take. Not only that, Ronald Colman began laughing uncontrollably at the ridiculousness of the scene. He continued laughing every time the shot was reattempted during the next three days. Finally, Herbert Brenon's threat to have the 1500 horses run over the actor stifled Colman's hilarity.

Beau Geste **(Paramount, 1926) Souvenir program cover**

An immediate hit, the film was one of the top moneymakers of the silent era and was named one of the year's Ten Best films by *The New York Times*. *Photoplay* magazine awarded it their Gold Medal as the Best Film of 1926. It was also ranked #5 on *Film Daily*'s Ten Best List for 1926. Like many major features, *Beau Geste* was originally road-shown. It also created some controversy when the French Consul protested the objectionable method used to advertise the film on the streets with men dressed in uniforms of the French Foreign Legion and wearing unauthorized decorations and orders. Glendon Allvine, Paramount's representative, said he had advertised for former Foreign Legion members to call for jobs at the theatre. The ten who responded were hired and the uniforms they wore were designed to be "pictorial duplicates" of the correct uniform. The consul was given tickets for opening night, but did not attend. Two other French officials did attend and favorably critiqued the film.

Beau Geste **(Paramount, 1926) Fort Zinderneuf**

The 1939 remake was to be a scene-for-scene effort by director William Wellman (1896–1975), but somewhere along the line things changed. Much of it is scene-for-scene, but the Marseilles sequence was cut for the film's 1950 re-release and a character was added for the early sequences at Brandon Abbas. Another difference is that the mutiny is planned in the barracks rather than at an oasis outside the fort. Other details vary; in the silent version, when Boldini is caught stealing and his fellow legionnaires punish him by running bayonets through his hands, he is shown from above with the bayonets through his palms; in the remake what happened is only suggested, and the thief's hands are shown bleeding. During the Arab siege, Sgt. LeJaune has the men bolster their spirits by singing the "Marching Song of the Legion" and by laughing. In the sound remake, they only laugh. In the silent version, Digby walks off alone into the desert at night (as in the book) so as not to be a burden to John and the two Americans. The 1939 version has him being shot by an Arab when he and John and the two American legionnaires attack a group of Arabs at an oasis.

Beau Geste (Paramount, 1939) J. Carrol Naish, Ray Milland, Gary Cooper, Brian Donlevy

There is little to be said of the 1966 version of *Beau Geste* save for its international cast, which lent credence to some of the more important roles and the use of actual ex-legionnaires as extras. The battle scenes were well handled, and Telly Savalas' (1924-1994) take on Sgt. LeJeune (here called Dagineau) is in keeping with the character, although he borrows Brian Donlevy's expression, "I promise you!" This version's Fort Zinderneuf was also more spacious than its predecessors. Despite using the same locations for the exteriors, the details of the story were so altered as to make the plot much less interesting. There are but two brothers, and they are Americans; Beau has fled to the Legion because of an embezzlement charge, so there is no mystery concerning a fabulous gem. The one superior element of this film is the photography, thanks mainly to the veteran eye of Oklahoman Bud Thackery (1903-1990). He began his career in 1924 at Warner Bros. while still a college student. He subsequently worked for RKO, First National, Paramount, Columbia and M-G-M before a twenty-six-year stint at Republic.

Beau Geste (Universal, 1966) Doug McClure, Guy Stockwell

Beau Geste became the first of a tetralogy of novels, to be followed by *Beau Sabreur* (1926), *Beau Ideal* (1928) and *Good Gestes* (1929). The second and third were adapted for the screen in 1928 and 1931 respectively; the fourth has never been filmed. *Beau Ideal* was also remade in Mexico in 1948 (see Chapter 7). *Beau Sabreur* utilized much unused footage from the first film and was made on half the budget. Veteran director James Cruze (1888?--1958) of *The Covered Wagon* (1923) and *Old Ironsides* (1926) fame and Paramount's top female star, blonde beauty Esther Ralston (1902-1994) were initially slated as members of the project. They were quickly replaced by William Wellman and dark-haired Evelyn Brent (1894-1975). Wellman, however, refused the job, as he correctly saw it as a bargain basement production. Having just helmed *Wings*, the picture which would win the first Best Picture Academy Award, he wanted to maintain his position as a director of "A" films. He was taken off the project and replaced by John Waters (1893-1965). Location shooting was done at Red Rock, California, and a desert area just north of Santa Barbara.

Beau Sabreur **(Paramount, 1928) Gary Cooper and Evelyn Brent**

Beau Sabreur fared only modestly at the box office; unfortunately, it is a lost film, so modern-day viewers are unable to judge it. *Beau Ideal* was made by a different studio, RKO, but Herbert Brenon again directed. The result left most critics unimpressed and was also a box-office failure. British actor Ralph Forbes (1902-1951) reprised his role of John Geste from the earlier picture. Wren's 1917 novel *Wages of Virtue* was the earliest of his works to be filmed, and also the first. Film legend Gloria Swanson (1897-1983) played the female lead, the biggest name of the silent era (except for Lillian Gish) to appear in a French Foreign Legion film.

Wages of Virtue **(Famous Players-Lasky-Paramount, 1924) Ben Lyon and Gloria Swanson**

Filmography

WAGES OF VIRTUE
Famous Players-Lasky-Paramount. Released November 10, 1924. 7 reels. Director: Allan Dwan. Presented by Adolph Zukor, Jesse L. Lasky. Scenario: Forrest Halsey, from the novel by P.C. Wren. Photography: George Webber. Cast: Gloria Swanson, Ben Lyon, Norman Trevor, Ivan Linow, Armand Cortez, Adrienne D'Ambricourt, Paul Panzer, Joe Moore.

New York Times, November 24, 1924: "Memories of brave little Cigarette in 'Under Two Flags' came to our mind...as we viewed Gloria Swanson's latest pictorial effort. Allan Dwan directed this picture which...is just as interesting as 'Manhandled,' his previous production with Miss Swanson."

Celebrated Sands: The Novels of P.C. Wren

Synopsis: A traveling show strongman named Luigi saves Carmelita from drowning and persuades her to team up with him. Later, in a fit of jealousy, Luigi kills his assistant, Giuseppe, and flees to Algiers with Carmelita. There, he enlists in the Foreign Legion and sets up the girl as owner of a café. An American legionnaire named Marvin falls for Carmelita, who has become the darling of the regiment. She stays loyal to Luigi from gratitude, however. Marvin is punished by the authorities after being framed for a crime by Luigi. In the ensuing battle between Luigi and Marvin, Luigi is holding the upper hand when Carmelita, who has discovered Luigi's plan to marry one Madame Le Cantiniere, stabs her savior. The legionnaires agree to attribute Luigi's death to an Arab and Marvin wins Carmelita.

BEAU GESTE

Paramount/Famous Players-Lasky. Released August 25, 1926. 10 reels. Director: Herbert Brenon. Producers: Adolph Zukor, Jesse L. Lasky. Scenario: Paul Schofield. Adaptation: John Russell, from the novel by P.C. Wren. Photography: J. Roy Hunt. Production Designer: Julian Boone-Fleming. Assistant Director: Ray Lissner. Production Superintendent: Frank Blount. Supervising Film Editor: Julian Johnson. Musical Score: Dr. Hugo Reisenfeld. Cast: Ronald Colman, Neil Hamilton, Ralph Forbes, Mary Brian, Noah Beery, Alice Joyce, William Powell, Victor McLaglen, Norman Trevor, Donald Stuart, Bernard Siegel, Paul McAllister, Maurice Murphy, Philippe DeLacey, Mickey McBan, Redmond Finlay, Ram Singh, George Regas.

New York Times, August 24, 1926: "Adventure, romance, mystery and brotherly affection are skillfully linked... Herbert Brenon...has succeeded in creating a remarkable degree of suspense. Noah Beery... gives an unforgettable performance as the tyrant, Sgt. LeJeune."

Variety, September 1, 1926: "The picture is all story. Scenically, 'Geste' is about the best example of desert shooting that has come along. J. Roy Hunt...has made an excellent job of it."

Synopsis: A Legion relief column approaches a fort. The commanding officer, Major Beaujolais, has his bugler blow a call. Receiving no response, he fires his pistol into the air, getting a rifle shot in return. Riding closer, he finds the wall manned by dead troops. The bugler volunteers to go in and open the gate for the column. When the gate remains closed after fifteen minutes, the major climbs in himself. On a parapet he finds a sergeant with a French bayonet in his chest and a dead legionnaire next to him. In the latter's hand is a note addressed to Scotland Yard--a confession for having stolen a fabulous sapphire, the "Blue Water," from Brandon Abbas in England. He calls for his bugler and again gets no reply, so he opens the gate himself. When he returns to the parapet, the bodies are gone. He decides to camp in the nearby oasis. The fort suddenly begins burning. The major sends two volunteers out for more men. The two American legionnaires, whom Beau and Digby had met at Marseilles, volunteer and set out. Fifteen years earlier, at Brandon Abbas, the Geste brothers--Beau, Digby and John--are playing with model ships on a pond. John is accidentally shot in the leg by cannon fire. Beau removes the bullet and gives his brother a "Viking funeral"--putting a toy sailor on ship with a figurine of a dog at his feet and setting the ship afire. Beau and Digby then promise to give each other Viking funerals depending on who dies first. Lady Brandon has two guests--an Indian and a Foreign Legion officer (Major

Beaujolais) to whom she shows the Blue Water. The major regales the boys with stories of the Legion. Needing money due to her absentee husband's gambling habits, Lady Brandon sells the Blue Water to the Indian, not knowing that Beau is hiding behind a suit of armor in the room. Years later, with the children grown up, Lady Brandon receives a telegram from her husband telling her to have the sapphire appraised and sold. Only Beau knows that she had replaced the real gem with a fake. That night at dinner, he asks to see the stone. While it is being shown, the lights suddenly go out. When they go back on, the gem is gone. Lady Brandon gives the thief a chance to return it by morning. Next morning it is still missing and so are the Geste brothers. Beau left a note for Digby, who left a note for John; both admitting to the theft. John leaves, too; Beau and Digby meet up at Marseilles, the enlistment port for the French Foreign Legion. Some time later, at Sidi-Bel-Abbes in Algeria, John turns up among the new recruits and is reunited with his brothers. There, a thief named Boldini overhears the brothers talking about the jewel. He tries to steal it from Beau, but is caught and punished by the other legionnaires. They hold him down on a bench and stick bayonets through his hands. Sgt. LeJaune breaks up the row and tells Boldini to tell him of any jewel thieves in the future. At Fort Zinderneuf the commanding officer dies and LeJaune takes over. His cruelty is so great that some of the legionnaires plan a mutiny in the oasis outside the fort. The Gestes and three others refuse to take part in it. LeJaune discovers the plot and uses those still loyal to help him suppress the mutiny. He's already called for relief, planning to tell them he quelled the mutiny himself so that he'll be called a hero. As he and the loyal legionnaires gather up rifles, Arabs attack and the company is forced to fight. LeJaune begins propping up dead legionnaires in embrasures to fool the Arabs into thinking that the legion force is stronger than it actually is. Between attacks, LeJaune has his men sing the "Legion Marching Song" and then orders them to laugh to make the Arabs think they are in good spirits. Beau is shot during the final attack. LeJaune orders John to bring him wine and bread. John tells him to leave Beau's body alone, but while he is downstairs, LeJaune rifles the corpse and retrieves Beau's confession. John sees this upon his return and threatens the sergeant, who pulls a gun on him and charges him with mutiny in the face of the enemy, for which the sentence is death. Beau is not dead yet, though; he trips LeJaune before he can fire and John stabs him with a bayonet. With his dying breath, Beau tells John to take the letter to Lady Brandon in England. It is then that the relief column seen at the beginning of the film arrives; it is John who fires back at the major before fleeing the fort. Digby is the bugler who volunteers to enter the fort. He gives Beau a "Viking funeral" with LeJaune as the "dog" at his feet; the flames consume the fort. Digby also leaves the fort and meets up with John a short distance from Zinderneuf. Later, they meet the two American legionnaires who had gotten lost on their mission. Five days later, with their water low and one of their camels dead, Digby sacrifices himself. He leaves a note for John and wanders off into the vast Sahara to die. John returns to England and Brandon Abbas alone, with Beau's confession, which he gives to Lady Brandon.

One of the very few silent Foreign Legion films extant, the rights to *Beau Geste* are owned by Paramount, which reportedly has no plans to release it on DVD. Should one wish to view it, one should check out local film archives. The Museum of Modern Art in New York owns a print. The composer of the music score, Dr. Hugo Riesenfeld, spent time in Paris selecting appropriate melodies and composed the score on his return trip aboard the *Leviathan*.

CELEBRATED SANDS: THE NOVELS OF P.C. WREN

BEAU SABREUR

Paramount. Released January 7, 1928. 7 reels. Director: John Waters. Scenario: Tom J. Geraghty, based on the novel by P.C. Wren. Photography: C. Edgar Schoenbaum. Second Cameraman: Henry Hollenberger. Film Editor: Rose Lowenger. Editor-in-Chief: E. Lloyd Sheldon. Assistant Directors: Charles Barton and Richard L. Johnson. Titles: Julian Johnson. Assistant Cameramen: Ralph Burdick, Lloyd Ahearn, Martin Cornica and Paul Lockwood. Cast: Gary Cooper, Evelyn Brent, Noah Beery, William Powell, Roscoe Karns, Mitchell Lewis, Arnold Kent, Raoul Paoli, Joan Standing, Frank Reichert, Oscar Smith, Alberto Morin.

New York Times, January 23, 1928: "Excellent direction, thoughtful casting and fine acting are contained in this offering. John Waters...permits his story to run....Gary Cooper's work as Maj. Beaujolais is splendid."

Beau Sabreur **(Paramount, 1928) Lobby card**

Synopsis: Legionnaires Henri de Beaujolais, Raoul de Redon and Dufour overstay their leave in Algiers and are thrown into jail. There, Henri earns the title "Beau Sabreur," given him by his uncle, General Beaujolais, when he wins a duel with a traitor named Becque. The general, who has plans for the Sahara, entreats Henri to forsake women for France, sending him first to the desert to learn the customs of the people, then to Zaguig, where he meets American journalist Mary Vanbrugh, whom he snubs, remembering his vow. Becque, hearing that Henri has orders to visit Sheikh El Hammel at a distant oasis to discuss a treaty, attacks Zaguig, hoping to prevent Henri's departure. Henri escapes with Mary, her maid and his aides. Out of distrust of Beque, the sheik agrees to a treaty with the French, and they resist an attack led by the vengeful Becque. Henri kills Becque in a duel. Having accomplished his task for France, he confesses his love for Mary.

BEAU IDEAL

RKO. Released January 25, 1931. 82mins. Director: Herbert Brenon. Producer: William LeBaron.   Screenplay: Paul Schofield, from the novel by P.C. Wren. Adaptation: Elizabeth Meehan. Photography: J. Roy Hunt. Music: Max Steiner. Assistant Director: Ray Lissner. Editor: Marie Halvey. Special Photographic Effects: Lloyd Knechtel. Scenery and Costumes: Max Ree. Recording: John E. Tribby. Dialogue: Marie Halvey. Cast: Lester Vail, Ralph Forbes, Don Alvarado, Loretta Young, Irene Rich, Otto Mattiesen, Paul McAllister, George Regas, Leni Stengel, Hale Hamilton, Frank McCormack, Bernard Siegel, Myrtle Stedman, Joseph DiStefani, John St. Polis. Remade in Mexico in 1947 as *Hermosa Ideal* (see Chapter 7).

Harrison's Reports, January 17, 1931: "...it is not... a very good entertainment, for very little appeal is directed to the emotions, and the action is not interesting enough to hold one's attention...."

Beau Ideal **(RKO, 1931) Arab cavalry charge**

Synopsis: A group of legionnaires, members of the penal battalion, are languishing in a desert grain pit; finally only two remain. As one of them nears death, he mutters the term "stout fellow" and is recognized by the other, his American friend Otis Madison, as John Geste. Their story is then told, beginning with their childhood friendship in the English countryside. Many years later, a grown Otis returns to England to propose to Isobel Brandon, the little girl whom both he and John adored as children. Otis is stunned to learn that John has joined the French Foreign Legion, where he was unjustly court-martialed and sentenced to a penal battalion. Moved by Isobel's tears, Otis pledges to rescue John, even though he knows Isobel is engaged to him. Otis changes his name to Brown when he joins the Legion and is sent to North Africa for training. On his first assignment, Otis' battalion is ordered to cross a stretch of the Sahara Desert on foot and occupy a French fort. Hit by a brutal sandstorm, some of the men buckle with exhaustion and mutiny. Although he tries to stop the uprising, Otis is accused of leading the mutiny and is sent to a penal battalion. Shortly after his arrival there, he suffers further punishment and thrown into the grain pit, where he finds John. A band of Arabs led by an emir and his half-French mistress, dancer Zuleika, rescues them. John is returned to the Legion as a prisoner, while Otis becomes a prisoner of the infatuated Zuleika, who informs him of an upcoming Arab revolt. By promising to take her to Paris, Otis gains his release from the dancer, who rides to alert the French cavalry. Disguised as an Arab, Otis sneaks into the French fort and joins the battle. Fighting side by side, John and Otis save the fort, thereby earning their freedom. True to his word, Otis prepares to leave John and return to Zuleika, but is relieved when he finds the fickle dancer in the arms of a Legion major.

Lester Vail (1899-1959) was loaned by M-G-M and Loretta Young (1913-2000) by First National for the leads in this production. The former replaced Douglas Fairbanks, Jr., who was recalled by Warner Bros. before shooting began. Location shooting was done in Mexico's Sonora Desert for two weeks. A box-office flop, the film lost over $300,000.

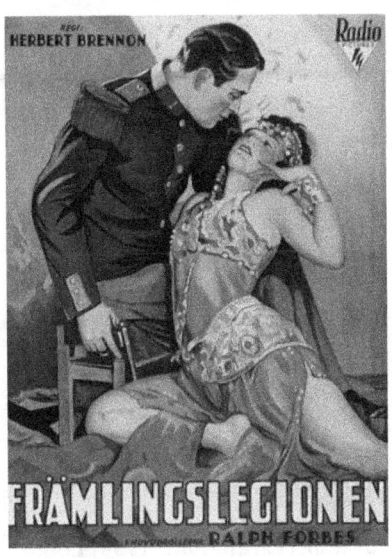

Beau Ideal (RKO, 1931) Swedish poster

BEAU GESTE

Paramount. Released August 2, 1939. 120mins. Producer and Director: William Wellman. Screenplay: Robert Carson. Photography: Theodore Sparkuhl and Archie Stout. Music: Alfred Newman. Art Direction: Hans Dreier, Robert Odell. Editor: Thomas Scott. Sound Recording: Hugo Gernsback and Walter Oberst. Costumes: Edith Head. Orchestral Arrangements: Edward Powell. Assistant Director: Joseph Youngerman. Second Unit Director: Richard Talmadge. Interior Decorations: A. E. Freudeman. Makeup: Wally Westmore. Technical Advisor: Louis Van Der Ecker. Cast: Gary Cooper, Robert Preston, Ray Milland, Brian Donlevy, Susan Hayward, J. Carrol Naish, Albert Dekker, Broderick Crawford, Charles Barton, James Stephenson, Heather Thatcher, G.P. Huntley, Jr., James Burke, Henry Brandon, Arthur Aylesworth, Harry Woods, Harold Huber, Stanley Andrews, Donald O'Connor, George Chandler, Billy Cook, Martin Spellman, David Holt, Ann Gillis, Harvey Stephens, Barry Macollum, Ronnie Randell, Frank Dawson, Duke Green, Thomas Jackson, Jerome Storm, Joseph Whitehead, Harry Worth, Nestor Paiva, George Regas, Francis McDonald, Carl Voss, Joe Bernard, Robert Perry, Larry Lawson, Henry Sylvester, Joseph William Cody, Joe Collins, Gladys Jeans, Bob Kortman, Gino Corrado. Academy Award Nominations: Best Supporting Actor (Brian Donlevy), Best Art Direction (Hans Dreier and Robert Odell).

Beau Geste (Paramount, 1939) Lobby card

New York Times, August 3, 1939: "...a mistake...to assume that the current generation will not find the current 'Beau' a stirring piece of cinema....Who stole that unparalleled sapphire, the 'Blue Water'? The question is still a gripping one."

***Beau Geste* (Paramount, 1939) Production shot at Fort Said**

***Beau Geste* (Paramount, 1939) The attack on Fort Zinderneuf**

Synopsis: Leading a relief troop of legionnaires to Fort Zinderneuf, Major de Beaujolais receives no response to his pistol shot. He sends his bugler to check out the situation. The bugler, Digby Geste, sends no sign, so the major goes inside himself. Upon entering the fort, he finds that all the defenders are dead, propped up in the embrasures with their weapons. He also finds a sergeant with a French bayonet in his chest and another dead legionnaire nearby. The corpse has a letter confessing to the theft of a fabulous sapphire from Brandon Abbey in England. A flashback to the abbey fifteen years earlier shows the Geste brothers being cared for by their Aunt Pat. They play at being soldiers, vowing to remain loyal to each other always, and for any survivor to give the other a "Viking funeral." Years pass, and the last valuable item of their uncle's estate, a magnificent sapphire known as "The Blue Water," is stolen one night after dinner. No one admits to the theft, but the next day, Beau Geste is gone and is followed by his brothers, all of whom join the French Foreign Legion. They all use assumed names, but a sneak thief learns that they are brothers and that they have a valuable jewel in their possession. He tells the cruel sergeant, who takes Beau and John with him to Fort Zinderneuf and assigns Digby to a different company. At Zinderneuf, the sergeant's cruelty leads to a mutiny which he puts down before it starts with the aid of the Gestes and two other legionnaires. As he begins a court-martial, Tuaregs attack the fort. All else is forgotten as the legionnaires begin their defense. They beat off two attacks, but their numbers decreases each time. The sergeant has the idea of propping up the dead to make it seem as if the fort is still fully manned. Finally, only two men remain, the sergeant and John Geste, Beau having been killed. The sergeant sends John to the kitchen for food; while he is gone, he searches Beau's body. John returns as he is doing this and threatens the officer, who pulls his pistol on him, charging him with mutiny in the face of the enemy. As he fires, Beau makes his final movement, tripping him, and John runs him through with a bayonet. John carries his brother's body to the barracks, where he places a flag over him and burns the body in a Viking funeral, using the body of Markoff for the "dog." He jumps over the wall when Major Beaujolais arrives. John, who has been hiding behind a dune, sees him and calls him over. Once the fire spreads, the major and his men adjourn to a nearby oasis. In the desert, the Gestes are joined by two American legionnaires who had been in their company and make their way home. On the way, however, they encounter some Tuaregs at an oasis; in attempting to scare them off by pretending to be a large force, Digby is killed. John returns to England alone.

Brian Donlevy's sneering and sadistic Sgt. Markov garnered an Academy Award nomination for Best Supporting Actor, while Hans Dreier and Robert Odell were nominated for their art direction. Six minutes were cut for the 1950 re-release; the shorter version is the only one available. This was to be Paramount's initial Technicolor film, and directed by Henry Hathaway (1898-1985) in 1936, but the large budget needed and the heat of the desert during summer changed the decision. Hathaway was given *The Trail of the Lonesome Pine* instead, which became the studio's first color effort.

Beau Geste marked the first credited role of Susan Hayward (1918-1975), who replaced Patricia Morison, as Isobel Rivers and who would become a major star in the following decade. Irish-born heavy Brian Donlevy (1902-1969) gave a memorable performance right from the start as he introduces himself to the new recruits: "I am Sgt. Markov. I make soldiers out of scum like you and I don't do it gently." With close-cropped hair and a facial scar, he backs up his statements by saying with a sneer: "I promise you." Later, during the final Arab attack, with legs akimbo, he urges on his men: "Rapid fire, you scum, rapid fire! Ha-ha!" A desert city was built 19 miles west of Yuma, Arizona, for the location shooting, in Buttercup Valley. The Imperial County Board of Supervisors renamed the site "Beau Geste Valley" while filming was in progress, but after the film crew left, the original name was reinstated.

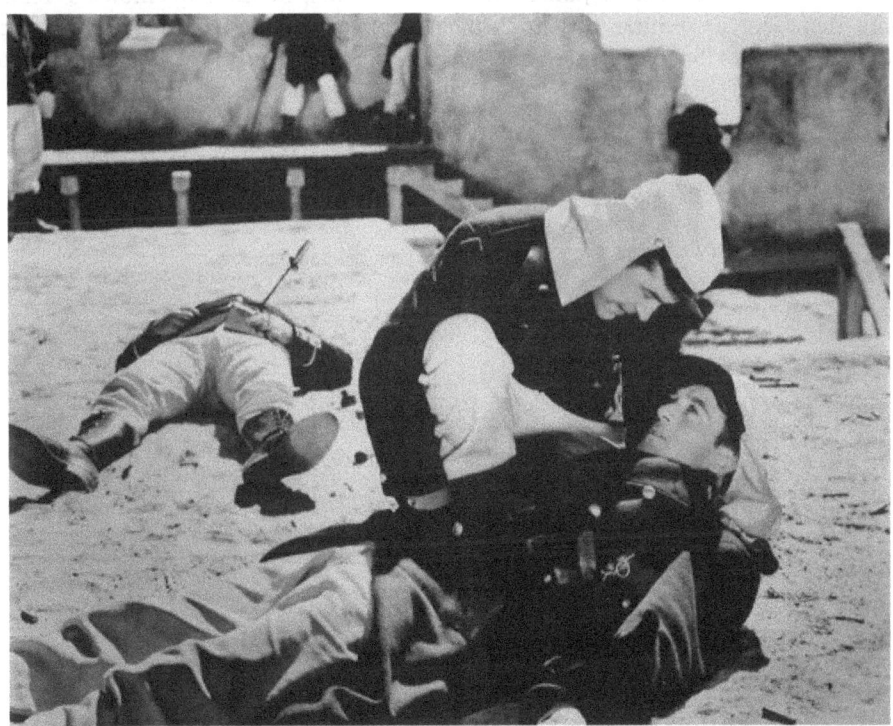

Beau Geste (Paramount, 1939) Ray Milland, Gary Cooper, Brian Donlevy with bayonet in chest in background

BEAU GESTE

Universal. Released September 7, 1966. 104mins. Color by Technicolor. Filmed in Techniscope. Director: Douglas Heyes. Producer: Walter Seltzer. Screenplay: Douglas Heyes, based on the novel by Percival Christopher Wren. Photography: Bud Thackery, A.S.C. Music: Hans J. Salter. Editor: Russell F. Schoengarth, A.C.E. Art Directors: Alexander Golitzen and Henry Bumstead. Set Decorations: John McCarthy and James S. Redd. Music Supervision: Joseph Gershenson. "Beau Geste March" by Hal Hopper. Makeup: Bud Westmore. Assistant Directors: Terry Morse, Jr., John Anderson, Jr. Unit Production Manager: Wes Thompson. Technical Advisor: O.R.O. Hatswell. Second Unit Director: Joe Kane. Sound: Waldon O. Watson, David H. Moriarty. Production Manager: James C. Pratt. Matte Supervisor: Albert Whitlock. Titles: Pacific Title. Costumes: Rosemary Odell. Cosmetics: Cinematique. Dialogue Coach: Rand Brooks. Stunt Coordinator: Hal Needham. Cast: Guy Stockwell, Doug McClure, Leslie Nielsen, Telly Savalas, David Mauro, Robert Wolders, Leo Gordon, Michael

Constantine, Malachi Throne, Joe DeSantis, X Brands, George Keymas, Patrick Whyte, Jeff Nelson, Ted Jacques, Michael Carr, Mario Roccuzzo, Dan Foster, Peter Sotos, David Gross, Hal Hopper, Chuck Wood, Duane Grey, Vic Lundin, Ava Zamora and the following former members of the French Foreign Legion: Arthur Atkinson, Albert Canter, Claude Chastanet, Boris Nico Dellwoy, Dimitri Drobatschewsky, John Du Mortier, Edward Erdmann, Antoine Figr, Frank Fuessler, Paul L. Jumet, Andrew G. Lontai, Maurice Malinowski, Yervand Markarian, George Olesnicki, Ulrich Schelling, Gunther Schumacher, Ernest Seidl, Francois Slistan, Douglas M. Smith, Charles Stransky, Henryk Szarek, Joseph Szepesy, Paul Villarose, Robert Vowels, Wesley T. Williams.

Variety, January 1, 1966: "...expertly made translation of P. C. Wren's novel...fine photographic values and fast direction...."

Beau Geste (Universal, 1966) Guy Stockwell finds himself in a grave situation

Silent Sands: Cinema de Legion, 1914–1928

Synopsis: In 1906, Beau Graves takes the blame for a crime committed by his business partner and leaves the United States to join the French Foreign Legion. He is sent to Fort Zinderneuf where he immediately runs afoul of the brutal and sadistic Sergeant-Major Dagineau, who suspects Beau of sending him an unsigned threatening letter. Beau wins the admiration of the other men, however, by standing up to Dagineau. He also wins the friendship of the weak and drunken commander Lt. De Ruse, who nicknames him "Geste" upon learning that Graves' sacrifice at home was unnecessary since his partner confessed and committed suicide shortly after Beau's departure. Later, Beau is joined by his devoted brother, John, and Dagineau becomes more convinced than ever that Beau plans to murder him. Lt. De Ruse is wounded by an Arab. Before dying, he confesses to Beau that it was he who wrote the anonymous letter to Dagineau in the hope that fear might make the sergeant more humane. The latter, driven to near madness by the prospect of sudden death, subjects his men to torturous marches and cruel punishments. As the Arabs launch a massive assault, the legionnaires are killed off one by one until only Dagineau and Graves remain. Beau wins the struggle between the two and is found by a relief column.

§

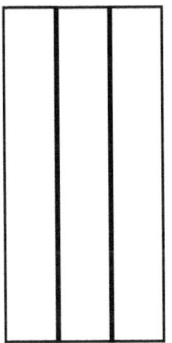

CHAPTER THREE
Silent Sands:
Cinema de Legion, 1914–1928

The silent era spawned a small number of other French Foreign Legion films, beginning around 1914. (See also Chapter 7.) Among them were two versions of a popular novel of 1911 entitled *The Red Mirage*, by a woman writer named Ida Alexis Ross Wylie. Both motion pictures used other titles. The first, produced by Lasky in 1915, was called *The Unknown*, and starred famed French actress Sarah Bernhardt's one-time lover, Lou Tellegen (1881-1934). The second was made near the end of the silent era in 1928 and called *The Foreign Legion*. Directed by Edward Sloman (1886-1972), it featured Lewis Stone (1879-1953), Mary Nolan (1905-1948) and Norman Kerry (1889-1956) in the lead roles. Unfortunately, both of these films are lost.

Two other popular writers of the day, Richard Harding Davis and A. E. W. Mason, had film adaptations made of their works. The former was represented by *Captain Macklin* (1915) and the latter by *The Winding Stair* (1925). Davis (1864-1916), a world-renowned reporter in his day almost totally forgotten now, is best known for his 1897 novel, *Soldiers of Fortune*. In *Captain Macklin*, he featured a flawed hero, a first for him, and sales suffered thereby. The film version was released in April 1915 and counted noted D. W. Griffith actress Lillian Gish (1893-1993) and future director Jack Conway (1887-1952) as the only players or technicians of note. Mason (1865-1948), an Englishman, was best known for his novels of empire, especially *The Four Feathers*, a 1902 novel that has been filmed seven times to date. *The Winding Stair* resulted from Mason's visit with the British Consulate in 1923. There, he was told stories of the Moorish revolt of April 1912. He coupled this with his experiences in the British Secret Service, writing the book very quickly; too quickly, as this writer found it quite dull. It was serialized in the *Grand Magazine* from February to August 1923.

Filmography

THE DISHONORED MEDAL

Reliance/Mutual. Released May 3, 1914. 4 reels. Director: W. Christy Cabanne. Supervisor: D. W. Griffith. Cast: Miriam Cooper, George Gebhardt, Raoul A. Walsh, Frank Bennett, Mabel Van Buren, Dark Cloud.

Variety, May 18, 1914: "The scenes are very effective, mostly exteriors and hence leading themselves to the best photographic results....there was shown some daring feats of horsemanship. The woman playing the dishonored Algerian girl had about as much expression as an Egyptian mummy. 'The Dishonored Medal' is a capital feature film."

Synopsis: In Algeria, a Legion lieutenant seduces a native girl, and then leaves her with their child and his medal of honor. The girl is befriended by a kindly sheik; when she is accidentally killed, the sheik raises her son as his own. The boy and the sheik's natural son become fast friends. In adulthood, they both fall in love with the same girl, who chooses the sheik's son. The lieutenant, now a general, returns to Algeria and lusts for the girl. He orders her to his tent, and the two friends lead a revolt for independence. Although they fare badly in battle, the two penetrate the general's headquarters, where the general's son fatally stabs his father. While dying, the general sees his medal of honor around his slayer's neck and realizes that the man is his son. The latter grinds the medal into the earth while he awaits his execution.

CAPTAIN MACKLIN

Majestic Motion Picture Co./A Mutual Masterpicture. Released April 22, 1915. 4 reels. Director: John B. O'Brien. Scenario: Russell E. Smith. Camera: H. B. Harris, based on the novel *Captain Macklin* by Richard Harding Davis. Cast: Jack Conway, Lillian Gish, Spottiswoode Aitken, W. E. Lowery, Dark Cloud.

Moving Picture World, May 1, 1915: "...is far the usual quality of feature pictures. The story is ... energetic and up to date, and has been smoothly carried in the picture."

Synopsis: Royal Macklin, who comes from a long line of American soldiers, is expelled from West Point. Determined to prove himself a good soldier, he journeys to Central America and joins the Foreign Legion under General Laguerre. The general makes him a captain due to his acquaintance with Macklin's grandfather, who had given his grandson a sword with which to fight for the family honor. Macklin becomes a strict disciplinarian and forms an effective fighting force. The revolutionary President Alvarez confiscates land owned by Macklin's uncle and arrests him and his daughter Beatrice. The uncle escapes and notifies Legion headquarters of what has transpired. Macklin leads an attack, retaking the capitol for the deposed General Garcia and rescues his cousin, whom he then marries, with his uncle's blessing.

SILENT SANDS: CINEMA DE LEGION, 1914–1928

THE UNKNOWN

Lasky. Released December 9, 1915. 5 reels. Director: George Melford. Scenario: Margaret Turnbull, from *The Red Mirage* by I. A. R. Wylie. Cast: Lou Tellegen, Theodore Roberts, Dorothy Davenport, Raymond Hatton, Hal Clements, Tom Forman, Horace B. Carpenter, George Gebhardt, Lucien Littlefield, Ramona the mule.

Variety, December 17, 1915: "...a stirring five-reeler...corking desert scenes...."

The Moving Picture World, December 4, 1915: "The production is lavish in detail."

Synopsis: Richard Farquhar, the ne'er-do-well nephew of a titled Englishman, finds himself penniless in an Algerian hotel after a binge. Instead of money from home, he gets a telegram stating that his allowance has been stopped and his uncle wants nothing more to do with him. He meets an American girl named Nancy Preston at a café. An Arab insults her; Richard goes to her aid and in the ensuing fight loses his father's Victoria Cross. Richard refuses to tell Nancy who he is until he has made a name for himself. He joins the Foreign Legion under an assumed name. He meets Nancy again and also Capt. Destinn. The latter falls in love with Nancy, but she prefers Richard. In the meantime, Richard's uncle has died and left him his entire estate. The family solicitor, while searching for the heir, meets Destinn and thinks he recognizes him as Richard's father. Destinn denies this. While pursuing Bedouins, Destinn's troop mutinies and ties him up, leaving him in the desert to die. Richard releases Destinn as the soldiers fight on; after the battle, Farquhar takes the blame for the mutiny and is sentenced to death. Nancy disguises herself as an Arab boy and helps Richard to escape. Fleeing into the desert, they are pursued by Destinn. When Richard discovers who his rescuer is, he gives her the Victoria Cross. Destinn recognizes it and allows the two to escape into British territory.

A SOLDIER OF THE LEGION

Universal Gold Seal. Released July 24, 1917. 3 reels. Director: Ruth Ann Baldwin. Story: R. A. Baldwin. Screenplay: Elliott J. Clawson. Cast: Irene Hunt, Leo Pierson, Grace Marvin, Noble Johnson, Violet Schramm, George C Pearce.

Moving Picture World, July 28, 1917: "...was shown as five reels, but will undoubtedly be cut to three. The manner of presenting this is light and fairly entertaining, but the subject as a whole has no strength, neither episode being entirely convincing."

Synopsis: Two young men with literary aspirations devise a story about a woman kidnapped by a Legion commandant's aide. The film's title is also the title of their story. The woman is rescued and returns to America. While the writers are out, the cleaning woman finds the manuscript and burns it on the stove.

The Unknown (Lasky, 1915) **Interior pages of herald**

THE MAN WHO TURNED WHITE

Jesse D. Hampton Prod./Robertson-Cole. Released June 1, 1919. 5 reels. Director: Park Frame. Producer: Jesse D. Hampton. Scenario: George Elwood Jenks. Story: F. McGraw Willis. Camera: William C. Foster. Cast: H. B. Warner, Barbara Castleton, Wedgewood Nowell, Carmen Phillips, Manuel Ojeda, Jay Dwiggins, Walter Perry, Eugenie Forde. (Re-released on May 15, 1922, by R-C Pictures as *The Sheik of Araby* and copyrighted under that title.)

Variety, June 13, 1919: "From beginning to end it is all story. The photography…is a continuous delight. The whole thing runs smoothly…."

Synopsis: Ali Zeman and his Bedouin band of robbers are the scourge of the merchants of Mzab who traversed the great Sahara Desert. The shrewd Ali has an able lieutenant in Joudar, the Bornu Berber, who was more implacable than Ali. Capt. Beverly of the Foreign Legion is enjoying a tryst with Ethel Lambert one night, unaware that Ali Zeman and his men are crawling across the sand toward them. Ali has come to kill Beverly, who had done him an irreparable wrong. He suddenly decides that the legionnaire would suffer more if his woman were taken from him. Beverly is knocked unconscious and Ethel is whisked away to the Arab's tent. Meanwhile, Joudar looks at the woman he has captured, comparing her to Ethel. He decides the latter is lovelier and henceforth desires only her. In a struggle with Ali, Ethel tears open his robe to reveal white skin. His latent chivalry aroused, Ali puts Ethel on his Arabian steed and directs her to the desert trail. An hour later, he too rides away over the silent sands. Fanina the dancer is the reason for the popularity of the "Ali Baba Café" in the lively town of Mzab. Beautiful even by Western standards, Fanina is considered a "Pearl of Paradise" in her sphere. But for none of the *habitués* does she have more than a smile and a teasing shrug of her lithe body since she had met Capt. Rand a few years ago. So when Capt. Rand enters the café, she greets him warmly. Beverly had told Rand's secret to Fanina and the jealous dancer is shrewd enough to guess that another woman is the reason for his returning to his real self. One evening in the café, Ethel, with her aunt and uncle, enter the wine shop, where they are set upon by some boisterous natives. Rand goes to their rescue, but is recognized by Ethel, who says nothing of their former meeting. At her invitation, however, he calls on her and in time their friendship ripens into love. When Beverly sees that Ethel is favoring Rand, he confronts Rand in her presence and tells Ethel that her lover had been dishonorably dismissed from the Legion on account of an affair with his colonel's wife. Furious, Rand chokes Beverly into unconsciousness, then apologizes to Ethel, but tells her he cannot explain. Meanwhile, Joudar, after his chief's desertion, swears that he will get the woman Ali has taken. Going to Mzab and learning of Fanina's jealousy of Ethel, he enlists her in his scheme to abduct her rival. As time passes, Ethel's love triumphs over her doubts. She sends a message by her servant to Rand, but it never reaches him. Rand, convinced that Ethel will never see him again, rides over the desert trail to the sea, with Joudar's band in hot pursuit. When Ethel learns that Rand did not receive her letter, she goes to his apartment. There, she meets Fanina, who gloatingly tells her that Rand has by now been captured by Joudar. In her rage, Fanina also tells Beverly what has occurred. Beverly sends word to the troops, and then rides furiously after Ethel, who has ridden out in the hope of warning Rand. Ethel reaches Rand after his horse has been shot from under him, and the two hide behind it as the Bedouins circle them. Beverly, through a hail of fire, joins them in their flight. The bandits draw closer; Beverly falls, mortally wounded. Dying, he confesses that he was the one responsible for Rand's disgrace and that Rand, out of gratitude to him for having saved his life, had borne the blame. The legionnaires arrive just as Joudar closes in on the trio and scatters his force over the desert. So Beverly finds a hero's grave in the desert and "The Man Who Turned White" returns to his heritage.

A SON OF THE SAHARA

Edwin Carewe Prod./Associated First National. Released April 13, 1924. 8 reels. Director: Edwin Carewe. Co-Director: René Plaisetty. Scenario: Adelaide Heilbronn, based on the book by Louise Gerard. Photography: Robert Kurn. Assistant Photographer: Al M. Greene. Art Director: John D. Schulze. Editor: Robert DeLacy. Assistant Director: Wallace Fox. Lab Technician: J. L. Courcier. Cast: Claire Windsor, Bert Lytell, Walter McGrail, Rosemary Theby, Marise Dorval, Montagu Love, Paul Panzer, Georges Chebat, Madame De Castilo.

Moving Picture World, May 31, 1924: "...was actually filmed in the great Sahara Desert. As a result, the atmosphere and locations are not only the real thing, but they add an unusual and distinctly pleasing appeal. The authentic backgrounds have been selected with an eye to the picturesque....the production is one that should fascinate the average patron...."

A Son of the Sahara (Edwin Carewe Prod./Assoc. First National, 1924)
Walter McGrail is the unlucky legionnaire

Synopsis: A boy named Raoul is raised by an Arab tribe. He grows into a refined Europeanized gentleman and falls in love with a European woman. She rejects his advances after learning of his background. Raoul captures her in a raid and then buys her at a slave auction. When she is rescued by legionnaires, Raoul's ancestry is established and he finds happiness with the woman.

LOVE AND GLORY

Universal-Jewel. Released December 7, 1924. 7 reels. Director: Rupert Julian. Story: Perley Poore Sheehan and Robert H. Davis. Scenario: Elliott Clowson and Rupert Julian, based on the novel *We Are French* by Percy P. Sheehan and R. H. Davis. Photography: Gilbert Warrenton. Cast: Madge Bellamy, Charles de Roche, Wallace MacDonald, Ford Sterling, Charles de Ravenne, Gibson Gowland, Priscilla Moran, Andre Lancy, Madame de Bodamere. Remake of *The Bugler of Algiers* (1916).

New York Times, August 11, 1924: "... some interesting scenes, beautifully photographed, which atone for certain defects....too much rhythm in the crowd scenes...."

Synopsis: Two French volunteers in the Algerian campaign become friendly rivals over the same girl. Before leaving for North Africa, one of them receives the girl's promise to await his return. Serving as a bugler, he is captured by the enemy and commanded to blow "Retreat."

He blows the "Charge" instead, and the French are victorious. Upon their return, the two friends find their village devastated by the Franco-Prussian war of 1870. Picard never tires of recounting his friend Emile's courageous exploit, until he finally becomes a laughing stock. He believes that if he repeats the story often enough, Emile will eventually receive governmental recognition. Years pass. Finally, the French government, in search of a hero, learns of Emile's deed and sends for him. Unwilling to desert his pal, Emile declines the offer of railroad transportation and sets out on foot with Picard for Paris. His strength gives out, however, and he dies en route. Picard changes uniforms with Emilo, borrows his credentials, assumes his identity and continues to Paris, where he receives Emile's decoration. The dead man's sweetheart is present at the ceremony and sees through Picard's deception. She keeps silent and accompanies him back to the body of Emile, upon whose tattered regimentals they reverently pin the long-awaited decoration.

While based on the same story as the earlier film, this version alters the French Army to the Foreign Legion.

THE WINDING STAIR

Fox. Released October 25, 1925. 6 reels. Director: Griffith Wray. Scenario: Julian LaMothe, from the novel by A. E. W. Mason. Photography: Karl Struss. Cast: Edmund Lowe, Alma Rubens, Warner Oland, Mahlon Hamilton, Emily Fitzroy, Chester Conklin, Frank Leigh, Captain Calvert, June Thomas.

Variety, January 20, 1926: "John Griffith Wray tried hard in the direction to get something into it that hadn't been done before, but even he could not find it...."

The Winding Stair **(Fox, 1925) Edmund Lowe with the gun**

Synopsis: A Foreign Legion officer falls in love with a native dancer at the infamous Iris Café in Morocco. He is ordered to put down an uprising by the Riffs, but discovers that the revolt is but a ruse to enable the natives to begin a massacre in the city. Ignored by his superiors, he disguises himself as a native, returns to the city and saves his lover and the Europeans there. Cast out as a deserter, he organizes a native regiment when the world war begins and, under an assumed name, offers their services to France. His heroism at Flanders' Fields restores both his citizenship and his honor. When wounded, he is rejoined by the dancer and they wed.

THE NEW COMMANDMENT

First National. Released November 1, 1925. 7 reels. Director: Howard Higgin. Presenter: Robert T. Kane. Screen adaptation: Sada Cowan, based on the novel *Invisible Wounds* by Frederick Palmer. Photography: Ernest Haller. Additional Photography: Ernest G. Palmer. Art Direction: Robert M. Haas. Editor: Paul F. Maschke. Cast: Blanche Sweet, Ben Lyon, Holbrook Blinn, Clare Eames, Effie Shannon, Dorothy Cumming, Pedro de Cordoba, George Cooper, Diana Kane, Lucius Henderson, Betty Jewel.

Variety, November 11, 1925: "...a little draggy in spots...about as good a picture as any of the average program features."

Synopsis: A scheming society woman tries to arrange a marriage between her stepdaughter and one Billy Morrow. She arranges for the man's father to take them on a cruise to Europe. Off the French coast, Morrow learns of the scheme and heads for shore with his friend, an ex-taxi driver. In Paris they meet an artist who is engaged to a countess, but in love with his model. Billy and the model fall in love, but he is suspicious of her intentions and of the artist. When war breaks out, Billy joins the Foreign Legion. He is wounded and taken to a hospital where the model is a nurse. There, they discover that they really care for each other.

THE SILENT LOVER

First National. Released November 21, 1926. 7 reels. Director: George Archinbaud. Screenplay: Carey Wilson, based on the play *Der Legioner* by Lajos Biro. Production Manager: Carey Wilson. Cast: Milton Sills, Natalie Kingston, William Humphrey, Arthur Edmund Carewe, William V. Mong, Viola Dana, Claude King, Charlie Murray, Arthur Stone, Alma Bennett, Montagu Love.

New York Times, November 15, 1926: "The director...impresses upon one the idea that if things are not as he pictures them in the Foreign Legion forts or on the sand, then they ought to be."

SILENT SANDS: CINEMA DE LEGION, 1914–1928

The Silent Lover (First National, 1926) Milton Sills

Synopsis: A dissolute count squanders his fortune in Paris, and then embezzles funds from an embassy while drunk. After all his money is gone, he contemplates suicide, but is persuaded to join the Foreign Legion instead. After long service there, he regains his honor and meets a rich American girl. She is touring Africa in the care of a faithless officer friend of the count. The officer involves the count in a military affair from which he can only be absolved by blaming a native girl who loves him. He thus hopes to retain the affections of the American girl. The outpost is attacked by desert tribesmen and the officer is forced to release the count. During the battle, the count and the American girl profess their mutual love. The native girl admits that the leader of the tribesmen is her father, and she is returned to him and the battle is ended.

THE FORBIDDEN WOMAN
Pathé Exchange/DeMille Pictures. Released November 7, 1927. 7 reels. Director: Paul L. Stein. Scenario: Clara Beranger, from *Brothers*, a story by Elmer Harris. Supervisor: William C. DeMille. Asst. Director: Curt Rehfeld. Photography: David Abel. Art Direction: Mitchell Leisen, Wilfred Buckland. Costumes: Adrian. Cast: Joseph Schildkraut, Jetta Goudal, Victor Varconi, Ivan Lebedeff, Leonid Snegoff, Josephine Norman.

Variety, November 2, 1927: "Exotic drama, with the emotional stuff laid on thick. The production is uncommonly beautiful and the acting graceful in spite of the stilted story....is a splendid bit of work on its technical side."

Synopsis: A beautiful spy for the Sultan of Morocco is commissioned to obtain military secrets from the French. The Sultan arranges a meeting between her and a French colonel. The pair marries and the woman thus obtains much valuable information which she transmits through her maid, who is also her accomplice. When the colonel is recalled to Paris, his wife joins him. There, she falls deeply in love with a renowned violinist. When she learns that he is her husband's younger brother, she despairs. They are caught in a compromising position and the violinist is sent to join the army in Morocco. Hopelessly in love with the younger man, the woman frames him as a spy, but his confession of love prompts her to admit her guilt and she is executed while the brothers watch.

THE FOREIGN LEGION

Universal. Released July 1 or September 23, 1928. 8 reels. Director: Edward Sloman. Scenario: Charles Kenyon, from a novel by I. A. R. Wylie, *The Red Mirage*. Titles: Jack Jarmuth. Photography: Jackson Rose. Editor: Ted Kent. Cast: Lewis Stone, Mary Nolan, Norman Kerry, Crauford Kent, Walter Perry, June Marlowe. Working Title: *The Red Mirage*.

Variety, June 27, 1928: "...extremely well made from a technical angle. It is in the story it falls down. Desert scenes splendid."

Motion Picture News, June 30, 1928: "...a fair picture as to plot and a good picture as to acting."

New York Times, June 25, 1928: "The background of the desert is finely photographed...and the story is quite well told."

***The Foreign Legion* (Universal, 1928) Lewis Stone bound for trouble (center)**

Synopsis: Richard, a young Englishman, is disgraced when he shoulders the blame for the actions of Arnaud, the husband of his former fiancée, Sylvia, a man-crazy woman. He enlists in the Foreign Legion under the command of his father, who is unknown to him. Arnaud and Sylvia, along with her sister, go to Algiers where they see Col. Destinn, Richard's father, punishing him for insubordination. Sylvia has an affair with Destinn and has her husband sent on a dangerous mission. Richard accuses Destinn of ungentlemanly conduct and the colonel takes his son with him to rescue Arnaud. In a severe sandstorm, Richard saves Destinn's life when the survivors of the troop try to kill him. They appoint Richard leader of the mutiny but Arnaud returns and arrests the men. At the trial, Destinn discovers that Richard is his son but is forced to sentence him to death. Sylvia's sister, Gabriella, who has been in love with Richard all along, tries desperately to save him and finally visits him in his cell, and is there when Destinn calls to bid his son goodbye. Arnaud shoots his wife and in the morning the firing squad arrests Destinn for liberating the prisoner. As they are escaping across the desert, Gabriella hands Richard a note from his father explaining about their kinship, but commanding him never to return to Algiers.

§

The Foreign Legion (Universal, 1928) Lobby card

CHAPTER FOUR
Sound Sands:
Cinema de Legion, 1929–2000

The industry-shaking advent of sound motion pictures in the late 1920s did nothing to halt the march of French Foreign Legion films. Almost a dozen Hollywood films featuring the Legion were produced in the first five years of sound movies alone, including three shorts and the only serial with a French Foreign Legion setting. Most of the major studios and several minor ones managed to turn out at least one motion picture featuring "the bravest of the brave."

Filmography

LOVE IN THE DESERT
FBO. Released March 17, 1929. 6 reels. Director: George Melford. Screenplay: Harvey Thew, Paul Percy. Story: Louis Sarecky. Dialogue: Harvey Thew. Photography: Paul Perry. Editor: Mildred Richter. Titles: Randolph Bartlett. Costumes: Walter Plunkett. Cast: Olive Borden, Hugh Trevor, Noah Beery, Frank Leigh, Pearl Varvell, William H. Tooker, Ida Darling, Alan Roscoe, Fatty Carr, Charles Brinley, Gordon Magee.

Variety, May 8, 1929: "Plenty of sand but not much excitement....Story is the usual desert stuff. The young American sap, sent to Arabia to keep away from the girls, is kidnapped. He is saved by Zarah, Arabian chieftain's daughter. That promotes a war. ...Preliminaries, introductions, overdrawn scenes and character delineations slow everything."

Synopsis: Bob Winslow, en route to his father's irrigation project underway in Northern Africa, is captured by an outlaw band commanded by Abdullah El Krish and held as hostage. In Abdullah's tent, he attracts the attention of Zarah, a native girl, and learns that she is the daughter of Harrim, a wealthy Arab who has come to Abdullah to intercede in behalf of the Winslow interests. Hating Abdullah because he has demanded her hand in marriage,

Zarah helps Bob to escape and permits him to ride with her party to Ourgla where the engineers have been anxiously awaiting his arrival. Abdullah is infuriated, and swearing vengeance, marshals his forces for an attack. To Harrim he sends the ultimatum that he must either surrender Zarah or the town will be sacked. Zarah, choosing to sacrifice herself rather than allow the impending massacre, goes to Abdullah's camp and gives herself up. As preparations are made for the wedding, Bob, with his friend Briggs, reaches the camp in disguise, overpowers the guards and escapes with Zarah. At dawn the next day, Abdullah's forces sweep down on the town but are checked at the gates by the gallant little band of legionnaires. Abdullah, putting a lieutenant in command, sets out in search of Zarah. He finds her defenseless in her father's house and she flees to the tower when Bob appears. In a terrific hand-to-hand struggle, Bob overpowers the Arab chief and hurls him over a parapet. News of their leader's death reaches the attacking tribesmen and they flee to the desert. Weeks later, word reaches Bob's parents in London that he is on his way home with a native bride. Horror-stricken, they have decided to disown him when he arrives with the beautiful Zarah and the news that she is really half-French and only recently out of school in London. So the parents' blessing comes to complete the happiness of the young couple.

This film has only 10% dialogue, being made at the end of the silent era. It appears that the sound scenes were added in the form of a prologue and epilogue.

TWO MEN AND A MAID

Tiffany-Stahl. Released June 15, 1929. 73mins. Director: George Archinbaud. Writers: Frederick Hatton, Fanny Hatton and Frances Hyland, from a story by John Francis Natteford. Photography: Harry Jackson. Music: Hugo Riesenfeld. Editor: Desmond O'Brien. Continuity: Frances Hyland. Dialogue/ Titles: Frederick and Fanny Hatton. Technical Advisor: Louis Van Der Ecker. Song, "Love Will Find You"--music and lyrics by L. Wolfe Gilbert and Abel Baer. Cast: William Collier, Jr., Alma Bennett, Eddie Gribbon, George E. Stone, Margaret Quimby. Released in both silent and sound versions, there are 17 minutes of sound in the latter.

Harrison's Reports, August 3, 1929: "The characters do nothing to arouse the sympathy of the spectator. On the contrary, they do things that arouse his antipathy."

Synopsis: An Englishman swears off women for life after he finds that there is another man in his wife's life. He joins the Foreign Legion to forget her and unwittingly becomes part of a love triangle at an outpost in Morocco. A café girl is loved by the company adjutant and she flirts with the Englishman. Eventually she develops real love for him. Their secret meetings are discovered by the adjutant, calling for a showdown between the two men. The girl sacrifices her life for the younger man, her true love.

WOMEN EVERYWHERE

Fox. Released June 1, 1930. 82mins. Director: Alexander Korda. Producer: William Fox. Associate Producer: Ned Marin. Story: Harlan Thompson, Lajos Biro. Music: William Kernell. Photography: Ernest Palmer. Sets: William Darling. Editor: Harold Shuster. Asst. Director: Edwin Marin. Wardrobe: Sophie Wachner. Sound Recording: Arthur L. von Kirbach. Songs: "Women Everywhere," "Beware of Love," "Marching Song," "Good Time

Fifi," "Bon Jour," "All in the Family," "Smile, Legionnaire." Cast: Fifi D'Orsay, J. Harold Murray, George Grossmith, Rose Dione, Clyde Cook, Ralph Kellard, Harlan Thompson, Walter McGrail. Working Title: *Hell's Belles*.

Women Everywhere (Fox, 1930) Fifi D'Orsay, J. Harold Murray. Walter McGrail

Variety, June 25, 1930: "...is one of those gems occasionally found in the herd of program pictures. ... this Fox film is excellent in all departments. Miss D'Orsay does more to establish herself as the female Chevalier than in any other work."

New York Times, January 23, 1930: "...a dawdling but often interesting audible pictorial story. ...Alexander Korda...succeeds in revealing his usual careful and imaginative direction."

Synopsis: An American gun-runner tries to escape from the Legion by hiding out in a nightclub in Casablanca where he meets a seductive singer. They fall in love, but the villain reappears and makes love to the woman, though she despises him. The villain becomes aware of the gun-runner's presence and threatens to expose him unless the singer marries him. The man finds a dead legionnaire and dons his uniform, but is picked up by a patrol and ordered to report to his regiment. He is then sent into the desert with the regiment where he distinguishes himself in a battle with the Arabs, but is wounded. He is returned to Casablanca and reunited with the singer. The villain finds him and again threatens to turn him in, but the man is shanghaied by the gun-runner's pals.

HELL'S ISLAND

Columbia. Released July 16, 1930. 77mins. Director: Edward Sloman. Producer: Harry Cohn. Story: Thomas Buckingham. Adaptation and Dialogue: Jo Swerling. Photography: Ted Tetzlaff. Editor: Leonard Wheeler. Art Director: Harrison Wiley. Asst. Director: C. C. Coleman. Sound Recording Engineers: G. R. Cooper, John Livadary. Cast: Jack Holt, Ralph Graves, Dorothy Sebastian, Richard Cramer, Harry Allen, Lionel Belmore, Otto Lang, Carl Stockdale.

Variety, July 23, 1930: "Interesting story...nice little bits all the way through, due to Sloman's direction ...there is something substantial to the picture...."

Harrison's Reports, July 19, 1930: "A strong melodrama...The interest is kept well. There is also strong love interest. Some thrills are offered by the fights between the French and the Riff."

Hell's Island (Columbia, 1930) Ralph Graves, Dorothy Sebastian, Jack Holt

Synopsis: Two Americans serving in the French Foreign Legion have become very good friends through shared experiences over the years. When they both meet a cabaret singer, their friendship becomes a serious rivalry. During a fight with the Riffs, one of them is shot in the back by a Riff sniper, but thinks his comrade has done it. The friend disobeys orders and stays with his wounded friend, resulting in a ten-year sentence on Devil's Island. The singer hears of their situations and concocts a scheme after learning that a legionnaire may serve out his enlistment as a prison guard and take his wife with him. When the wounded friend is released from the hospital, she tells him that his friend has left her and he proposes to her. When they arrive at the prison colony, he spots his friend among the prisoners and realizes he has been tricked. The singer confesses. Her husband says he will help his friend to escape, while secretly plotting revenge for the shot in the back. The plan is have the friend escape and meet the woman in a launch, when he will shoot the friend with the same bullet that almost killed him. A fellow legionnaire sees him trying to load the spent cartridge into his rifle and tells him it can't be done for it was made for a Riff gun. He has a change of heart and decides to help his friend escape with the woman. His friend's escape has been discovered, however, so he catches up with them and exchanges clothes with his friend and is shot by guards. His friend and the woman get away safely.

RENEGADES

Fox. Released October 26, 1930. 84mins. Director: Victor Fleming. Producer: William Fox. Screenplay: Jules Furthman, from the novel by André Armandy. Photography: L. William O'Connell. Costume Design: Sophie Wachner. Editor: Harold Shuster. Set Decorator: William Darling. Asst. Director: William Tummel. Technical Advisor: Louis Van Der Ecker. Cast: Warner Baxter, Myrna Loy, Noah Beery, Bela Lugosi, C. Henry Gordon, Gregory Gaye, George Cooper, Colin Chase, Noah Beery, Jr., Fred Kohler, Jr., Victor Jory, Noble Johnson.

Renegades (Fox, 1930) **Warner Baxter, Myrna Loy, Bela Lugosi**

Variety, November 12, 1930: "...some exciting fight scenes and good performances....Miss Loy in spots is inclined to be recitational. This gives a certain stagy atmosphere which abets unconvincing qualities."

New York Times, November 8, 1930: "...is endowed with impressive desert scenes and capable acting....a muddled and tedious offering."

Synopsis: Four legionnaires are first insubordinate and then become deserters. They join their heathen enemies, where one of them meets a former lover, who has also converted. While her hatred of him is apparent, he still protects her from abuse by the Arabs. The four deserters later have a change of heart and turn on the Arabs when the latter besiege a Legion fort.

MOROCCO

Paramount. Released December 6, 1930. 90mins. Director: Josef von Sternberg. Scenarist: Jules Furthman, based on the novel *Amy Jolly* and *The Woman from Marrakesh* by Benno Vigny. Photography: Lee Garmes. Editor: Sam Winston. Art Director: Hans Dreier. Costumes: Travis Banton. Songs: "Give Me the Man," "What Am I Bid for My Apples" by Leo Robin and Karl Hajos, "Quand L'Amour Meurt" by Cremieux and Millandy. Cast: Marlene Dietrich, Gary Cooper, Adolphe Menjou, Ulrich Haupt, Juliette Compton, Francis McDonald, Albert Conti, Eve Southern, Michael Visaroff, Paul Porcasi, Emile Chautard, Theresa Harris. Academy Award Nominations: Best Director (Josef von Sternberg); Best Cinematography (Lee Garmes); Best Actress (Marlene Dietrich).

Morocco **(Paramount, 1930) Gary Cooper and Marlene Dietrich**

Sound Sands: Cinema de Legion, 1929–2000

Morocco (Paramount, 1930) Magazine ad

Variety, November 19, 1930: "...'Morocco' is too lightweight a story to be counterbalanced by the big-time direction given it....von Sternberg is trying all the time to stir up some action and liveliness in the proceedings. ...he accomplishes this in part mainly by the marching troops..."

Harrison's Reports, November 29, 1930: "A fairly entertaining picture; it rises above just the ordinary because of...Marlene Dietrich, who is interesting and gives a fine performance. The story ... lags as does the dialogue."

Synopsis: A singer arrives in a Moroccan city and becomes the headliner at a cabaret. There, she falls for a legionnaire who is suspected of an indiscretion with an adjutant's wife. She alibis for him when both are called before the adjutant, and they are released. The legionnaire is sent on a dangerous mission after telling the singer he wishes to quit the Legion. He changes his mind and she accepts the offer of marriage from a wealthy artist whom she had met on board ship. When the soldier's patrol returns, the singer must be assured that he is alive before marrying the artist. She searches everywhere for him and finally finds him with a native woman in a cheap dive. He tells her he no longer cares for her, but she notices that he has carved her name on a table. The next day the soldier's company prepares to move to another base. Seeing some women following the troops, the singer discovers that they follow their men wherever they go. She suddenly removes her shoes and goes off with them.

This was German actress Marlene Dietrich's (1901-1990) first American film and her sole Academy Award nomination.

OUTPOSTS OF THE FOREIGN LEGION

Educational Productions. Released 1931. Color. Director: Harry Perry.

THE FRENCH FOREIGN LEGION

Fox Magic Carpet Series. Released November 1931. 10mins. Documentary short.

Synopsis: The Legion is shown building railroads across the desert as well as marching to military tunes, played by their own symphony orchestra.

WITH THE FOREIGN LEGION

Fox. Released January 10, 1932. 10½mins. Documentary short.

THE THREE MUSKETEERS

Mascot. Released April 7, 1933. 12-chapter serial. Directors: Armand Schaefer and Colbert Clark. Story: Norman Hall, Colbert Clark, Ben Holm, Wyndham Gittens and Barney Serecky. Photography: Ernest Miller and Tom Galligen. Supervising Editor: Wyndham Gittens. Editor: Ray Snyder. Music: Lee Zahler. Dialogue: Ella Arnold. Asst. Cameramen: Monte Steadman, Joe Lykens. Asst. Directors: George Webster and Louis Germonprez. Sound Engineer: Homer Ackerman. Production Manager: Larry Wickland. Cast: Jack Mulhall, Raymond Hatton, Francis X. Bushman, Jr., John Wayne, Ruth Hall, Creighton Chaney, Hooper Atchley, Gordon DeMain, Robert Frazer, Noah Beery, Jr., Al Ferguson, Edward Peil,

Sr., William Desmond, George Magrill, Emile Chautard, Robert Warwick, Wilfred Lucas, Yakima Canutt, Rodney Hildebrandt.

Chapter Titles:
1. *The Fiery Circle*
2. *One for All and All for One*
3. *The Master Spy*
4. *Pirates of the Desert*
5. *Rebel Rifles*
6. *Death's Marathon*
7. *Naked Steel*
8. *The Master Strikes*
9. *The Fatal Circle*
10. *Trapped*
11. *The Measure of a Man*
12. *The Glory of Comrades*

The Three Musketeers (Mascot, 1933) **John Wayne, Robert Frazer**

The Three Musketeers (Mascot, 1933) Ruth Hall, Hooper Atchley, Raymond Hatton, Jack Mulhall, Francis X. Bushman, Jr., George Magrill

Synopsis: Three Legionnaires and an American army pilot battle the forces of "The Devil's Circle," a secret society led by one El Shaitan. After his identity is exposed by them, El Shaitan tries to kill the pilot but is shot by the others.

Shot in Yuma, Bronson Canyon and Griffith Park, Hollywood. Feature version, *Desert Command*, released by Favorite Films in 1949. This is the third and last serial in which film legend John Wayne (1907-1979) appeared.

THE DEVIL'S IN LOVE

Fox. Released July 21, 1933. 70mins. Director: William Dieterle. Writer: Howard Estabrook, from a story by Harry Hervey. Photography: Hal Mohr. Editor: Ralph Dietrich. Cast: Victor Jory, Loretta Young, Vivienne Osborne, David Manners, C. Henry Gordon, Herbert Mundin, J. Carrol Naish, Emile Chautard, John Davidson, Akim Tamiroff, Bela Lugosi, Robert Barrat, Dewey Robinson, Francis MacDonald.

Variety, August 1, 1933: "Victor Jory and Loretta Young do a good job and with support around them will please the average fan."

New York Times, July 29, 1933: "...there is nothing especially remarkable about the picture....a slightly changed version of an old story...."

Harrison's Reports, August 5, 1933: "The background is colorful and there is fast action in some of the warfare scenes."

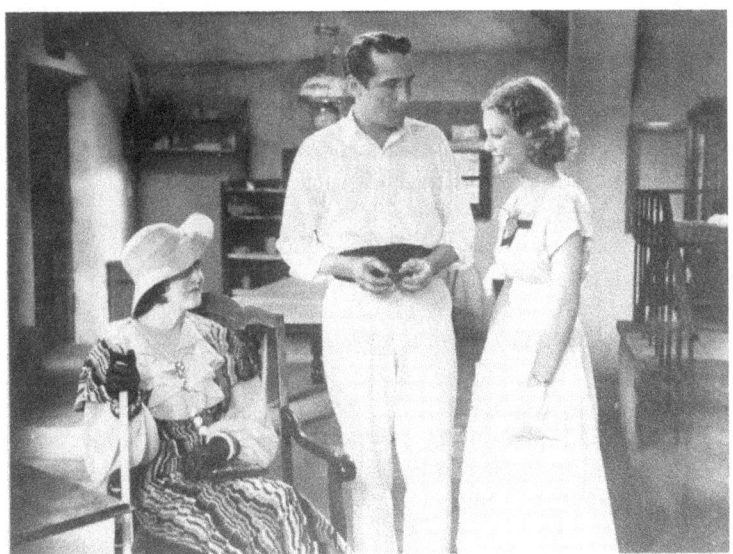

The Devil's in Love (Fox, 1936) Vivienne Osborne, Victor Jory, Loretta Young

Synopsis: A Legion doctor is falsely accused of murdering the commandant of Fort Roudet. Sentenced to be executed, he manages to escape to Port Zamba, where he establishes a practice. There, he meets and falls in love with a woman who is engaged to a captain at Fort Roudet. He agrees to escort her to see him. When they arrive, they find the fort besieged by Arabs. The latter are driven off by four French planes. The captain is killed and the real murderer discovered.

THE LEGION OF MISSING MEN

Monogram. Released July 28, 1937. 63mins. Director: Hamilton McFadden. Producer: I. E. Chadwick. Story: Norman S. Hall. Photography: Marcel Le Picard. Scenario and Dialogue: Sherman L. Lowe and Harry O. Hoyt. Settings: Fred Preble. Supervisor: Charles Hutchison. Songs: Richard Gump and Flo Browne. Cast: Ralph Forbes, Ben Alexander, Hala Linda, George Regas, James Aubrey, Paul Hurst, Frank Leigh, Roy D'Arcy.

Variety, September 22, 1937: "Action shots are library, film is jumpy in the outdoor sequences and sound not much better."

Synopsis: A Legion company carrying machine guns to a fort is ambushed by tribesmen and the machine guns captured. The local café singer is considered to be the sergeant's woman, though she cares for an enlisted man. The latter is not interested in her; when his younger brother suddenly appears in the Legion, he falls hard for the singer and begins spending time with her. When the sergeant finds them together, he calls the woman a tramp and the legionnaire punches him. For striking a superior, he is to be sent to a penal battalion. The singer helps him escape with the aid of two tribesmen, for she is also friendly with the sheik. His brother and another legionnaire take him back from the tribesmen, killing one in the process, but are captured by a group of Arabs and taken to the sheik. The sheik has the machine guns, but doesn't know how to assemble them. He tortures the younger brother and tells the older one he will be killed unless the legionnaire assembles the guns and helps the sheik in his attack upon the fort. The legionnaire agrees, but files down a particular piece on some of the guns so that they will not work after firing a few rounds. He also tells the singer that she must ride to warn the Legion of the forth coming attack. She does, and a relief troop arrives at the fort in time to help beat back the sheik's forces.

TROUBLE IN MOROCCO

Columbia. Released March 9, 1937. 62mins. Director: Ernest B. Schoedsack. Producer: Larry Darmour. Screenplay: Paul Franklin. Story: J. D. Newsom. Photography: James Brown. Cast: Jack Holt, Mae Clarke, C. Henry Gordon, Harold Huber, Oscar Apfel, Bradley Page, Victor Varconi, Paul Hurst.

Variety, March 17, 1937: "Producers expended real coin for production, extras and atmospheric backgrounds, yet the editing plainly indicates they regarded this as little more than a programmer....Holt contributes a nicely paced job as the scribe..."

Synopsis: Two foreign correspondents investigate an arms smuggler in Cairo. One of them becomes involved with a gangster who mistakes him for another crook and he joins the Foreign Legion, where he finds himself battling desert tribesmen.

Trouble in Morocco (Columbia, 1937) Jack Holt, Victor Varconi

Sound Sands: Cinema de Legion, 1929–2000

ADVENTURE IN SAHARA

Columbia. Released November 23, 1938. 59mins. Director: D. Ross Lederman. Producer: Louis B. Appleton. Story: Sam Fuller. Screenplay: Maxwell Shane. Photography: Franz Planer. Music Direction: M. W. Stoloff. Editor: Otto Meyer. Cast: Paul Kelly, C. Henry Gordon, Lorna Gray, Robert Fiske, Marc Lawrence, Dick Curtis, Stanley Brown, Alan Bridge, Raphael Bennett, Charles Moore, Dwight Frye, Stanley Andrews, Edwin Stanley, Al Herman, Rolfe Sedan, Blackie Whiteford, James Millican, Jean DeBriac, Boyd Irwin Sr., Sherry Hall, Harry Strange, George Chesebro, Albert Pollet, George Ducount, Jack Lowe.

Variety, December 21, 1938: "Film's brevity is its prime virtue....exceptionally poor dialog.... flock of stock and duplicate running shots."

Synopsis: A regiment of legionnaires mutinies against their cruel commander, stranding him and a few loyal followers in the desert with meager supplies. He vows revenge. When he and his men return to the fort, they find it under attack by Arab tribesmen. The mutinous soldiers take him back and together they defeat the Arabs. The leader of the mutineers is given a medal for his bravery, but is later court-martialed. The commander's cruelty is exposed at the trial.

Adventure in Sahara (Columbia, 1938) Paul Kelly, Dick Curtis, Lorna Gray

DRUMS OF THE DESERT

Monogram. Released October 7, 1940. 64mins. Director: George Waggner. Producer: Paul Malvern. Screenplay: Dorothy Reid and Joseph West (George Waggner). Original Story: John T. Neville. Photography: Fred Jackman, Jr. Editor: Jack Ogilvie. Music: Edward Kay. Technical Director: Charles Clague. Sound Direction: William Fox. Interior Decorations: David Milton. Cast: Ralph Byrd, Lorna Gray, Mantan Moreland, George Peter Lynn, Willie Castello, Jean Del-Val, Ann Codee, Boyd Irwin, Neyle Marx, Alberto Morin, Charles Townsend, Jack Chefe, John Stark, Bud Harrison.

The Exhibitor, October 16, 1940: "...one of the better action offerings from Monogram...."

Synopsis: Lt. Paul Dumont of the French Foreign Legion is assigned to command Senegalese paratroopers. On board ship, he meets a young woman to whom he becomes attracted. At the Legion post, he meets his old friend, Capt. Jean Renault, only to discover that the young woman is his fiancée. At their training base, the troops are attacked by an Arab force. The captain is wounded, though saved by Dumont. The leader of the Arabs is captured by the paratroopers. He is tried and condemned to death. His older brother, a sheik, vows vengeance after his brother is executed by a firing squad. Dumont and the girl fall in love. They are later captured by the sheik. When Capt. Renault learns of this, he sneaks into the Arab camp, only to be captured. The Senegalese paratroopers come to the rescue, routing the Arabs, but Capt. Renault is mortally wounded. Before dying, he gives his blessing to Lt. Dumont and his fiancée.

FORT ALGIERS

United Artists. Released July 15, 1953. 78mins. Director: Lesley Selander. Producer: Joseph N. Ermolieff. Assoc. Producer: Edward L. Alperson, Jr. Story: Frederick Stephani. Screenplay: Theodore St. John. Photography: Charles Lawton, Jr. Music: Michel Michelet. Editor: Jerome Thoms. Art Direction: Boris Leven, Robert Peterson. Gowns: Yvonne Wood. Song: "I'll Follow You" by Michel Michelet and Yvonne De Carlo. Cast: Yvonne De Carlo, Carlos Thompson, Raymond Burr, Leif Ericson, Anthony Caruso, John Dehner, Robert Boon, Henry Corden, Joe Kirk, Bill Phipps, Sandra Gale, Charles Evans.

Harrison's Reports, July 18, 1953: "A routine program melodrama, undistinguished in writing, direction and acting. The story...is rather dull and uninteresting."

Exhibitor, July 29, 1953: "Composed of familiar elements and devoid of any particular luster...."

Synopsis: A French cabaret singer attempts to expose an Arab leader who is planning an attack against the French. She tries to seduce him in his palace, but her identity is discovered and she must be saved by her lover, a Foreign Legionnaire.

Sound Sands: Cinema de Legion, 1929–2000

Fort Algiers (United Artists, 1953) Title card

DESERT LEGION

Universal. Released May 8, 1953. 86mins. Technicolor. Director: Joseph Pevney. Writers: Irving Wallace and Lewis Meltzer, from the novel *The Demon Caravan* by George A. Surdez. Photography: John Seitz. Art Direction: Alexander Golitzen, Robert Clatworthy. Music: Frank Skinner. Editor: Frank Gross. Choreography: Asoka. Cast: Alan Ladd, Richard Conte, Arlene Dahl, Akim Tamiroff, Leon Askin, Oscar Beregi, Anthony Caruso, Ivan Triesault, Don Blackman, Dave Sharpe, Ted Hecht, George J. Lewis, Pat Lane, Elsa Edsman, Sujata, Asoka, Henri Letondal, Peter Coe.

New York Times, May 9, 1953: "...impossibly dull...action romance"... Joseph Pevney directed competently..."

Exhibitor, March 11, 1953: "Packed with action, attractive color, the lure of the Legion, Ladd in a typical role and a gorgeous Dahl....it is all done in a workmanlike manner..."

Synopsis: A Legion outpost in Algeria is bedeviled by Ben Omar Khalif and his band, who ambush Legion detachments and disappear. After one such ambush, the Legion officer in command is found and taken to a hidden city in the mountains nearby. He awakens to find himself being tended by a redheaded beauty who refuses to tell him anything. When he returns to his post, no one believes him about the woman. Burning with a desire to avenge his lost troops, the officer tries to find the hidden city against orders. In a native village, he is met by one of the residents of the city who takes him and his corporal there. In the city he meets the old ruler and his lieutenant. The old ruler turns out to be a former

Desert Legion (Universal-International, 1953) Poster

Legionnaire who had deserted the Legion many years before after killing a man. The woman is his daughter; he had founded the city as a buffer between the tribes and the French. He tells the officer that the peace is threatened by factions formed by his lieutenant, who is later revealed as Ben Omar Khalif and is challenged to a duel by the officer. Neither wins, but the officer and his corporal are held prisoner while Khalif plans a final assault against the French. With the aid of the old legionnaire and his daughter, they escape with arms and ride to the pass as Khalif's men are ambushing a Legion company. They turn the tide of battle, Khalif is killed, and the officer returns to the city and the woman.

LEGIONNAIRE

E. P. Pressman Film Corp./Lions Gate Films (U.S.). Released February 9, 1999 on video. 90mins. Director: Peter MacDonald. Producers: Christian H. Solomon, Edward Pressman, Kamel Krifa, Sheldon Lettich, Peter MacDonald, Roberto Malerba, Jean-Claude Van

Legionnaire (Pressman Film/Lion's Gate, 1999) DVD cover

Damme, Richard G. Murphy, Gregory G. Woertz. Photography: Douglas Milsome. Story: Sheldon Lettich, Jean-Claude Van Damme. Screenplay: Sheldom Lettich and Rebecca Morrison. Editors: Mike Murphy, Christopher Tellefsen. Production Design: Charles Wood. Art Direction: Marco Trentini. Production Manager: Fabiomassimo Dell'Orco. Makeup: Katalin Elck. Hair Stylist: Alberto Moccia. Second Unit Director: Mike Brewster. Original Music: John Altman. Cast: Jean-Claude Van Damme, Adewale Akinnuoye-Agbaje, Steven Berkoff, Nicholas Farrell, Jim Carter, Ana Sofrenovic, Daniel Caltagirone, Anders Peter Bro, Tom Delmar, Pilly de Vicente, Amrani Hanfine, David Hayman, Mario Kalli, Rob Kaman, Kamel Krifa, Paul Kynman, Derek Lea, Joseph Long, Joe Montana, Vincent Pickering, Kim Romer, Kelli Shaughnessy, Andy Smart, Takis Triggelis, Charles J. H. Wood. Opened initially in Europe, and released on video prior to theatrical release in the United States. Filmed on location in Morocco.

New York Times, January 8, 1999: "...the film resembles action adventures of the '40s and '50s...."

Synopsis: In 1925, a Marseilles playboy becomes involved with a mobster's girlfriend and also fails to throw an amateur boxing match after being paid by the mobster to do so. While fleeing, he accidentally causes the death of the mob boss' brother. He joins the Foreign Legion to escape the gang revenge. He is sent to Morocco in the midst of the Riff war. As part of a platoon sent to reinforce a nearly ruined fort, he becomes the sole survivor of a Riff attack. The Riff allow him to live due to his bravery and he is told to tell the French that they can expect more of the same if they continue to invade his country.

§

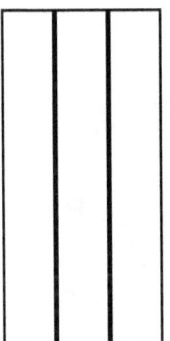

CHAPTER FIVE
Singing Sands:
Legion Musicals

Unique among French Foreign Legion films are the four versions of one of the few musicals with a Legion setting, *The Desert Song*, and an early sound version of a Victor Herbert operetta entitled *Mademoiselle Modiste*. The stage version of *The Desert Song* opened on Broadway November 30, 1926, and ran for 471 performances. Presented in two acts and eight scenes, the score was by top operetta composer Sigmund Romberg, while Otto Harbach, Oscar Hammerstein II and Frank Mandel wrote the book. Directed by Arthur Hurley, it had musical numbers staged by Robert Connolly and featured settings by Woodman Thompson. The original title was "Lady Fair." The critic for *The New York Times* opined, "It is all floridly contrived, and executed in the grand, unstinting manner..." He called Sigmund Romberg's score "excellent and rather imposing" and stated that "the stirring and resonant male chorus...provoked considerable enthusiasm." He closed by summing up the play as "...a large, slightly top heavy entertainment, providing full value for your money..." A ninety-minute television version was produced by NBC in 1955 (see Chapter 9).

Filmography

THE DESERT SONG
Warner Bros. Released April 10, 1929. 13 reels. (125mins.). Director: Roy Del Ruth. Screenplay: Harvey Gates, from the operetta by Otto Harbach, Laurence Schwab, Frank Mandel and Oscar Hammerstein II. Photography: Bernard McGill. Music: Sigmund Romberg. Editor: Ralph Dawson. Cast: John Boles, Carlotta King, Louise Fazenda, Johnny Arthur, Edward Martindel, Jack Pratt, Robert E. Guzman, Otto Hoffman, Marie Wells, John Miljan, Myrna Loy, Del Elliott.

Variety, April 3, 1929: "Taking another step forward in the talking field by doing an operetta, following the story in detail and getting in the entire musical score and compositions, Warner Brothers have another box office winner ... Mr. Boles and Miss King do exceptionally well on the screen...their conceptions of the film characters are sincere....Recording and photography excellent with color shots, though few, well chosen...."

The Desert Song (Warner Bros., 1929) Magazine ad

Synopsis: As the Red Shadow, a former Legion officer tells how he joined the French Foreign Legion to impress his lady love. Ordered by a general known as "The Butcher" to raid a Riff camp and kill everyone there, he is appalled by this brutal order and flees to another Riff camp where he forms a band to fight injustice. When he returns to French territory, he is forced to resign. He puts on an act as a buffoon. When his father, a general, becomes the governor upon the previous governor's death, he vows to bring the Red Shadow to justice. The man's lady also appears in Morocco. The father is ashamed of his son, not knowing his secret identity. A Riff dancing girl accidentally learns the Red Shadow's true identity. In love with a Legion captain, she offers to tell him if he'll give up the French woman he's been seeing, but he refuses. The Red Shadow kidnaps the French woman he loves and seeks shelter in the home of a sheik. As the buffoon, he learns that the woman now loves the Red Shadow. The dancing girl brings the general to the sheik's home, where the sheik agrees to let the French woman go if the general can defeat the Red Shadow in a duel. The Red Shadow refuses to fight because he doesn't want to harm his father, though only he knows that. He is exiled to the desert. The general orders his men to hunt down and kill the Red Shadow. While his men are out searching for the Riff leader, the general learns from the dancing girl that his son is the Red Shadow. His men return and tell him that the Red Shadow was killed by his son. The general privately tells his son that he is proud of him and forgives his actions as the outlaw. The son then reveals the truth to the French woman.

KISS ME AGAIN

First National. Released February 23, 1931. 76mins. Technicolor. Director: William A. Seiter. Screenplay: Julien Josephson and Paul Perez, based on the operetta *Mademoiselle Modiste* by Victor Herbert. Cinematography: Lee Garmes, Alfred Gilks. Editor: Peter Fritch. Art Direction: Anton Grot. Score: Henry Martyn Blossom. Costumes: Edward Stevenson. Dance Ensembles: Larry Ceballos. Vitaphone Orchestra Conductor: Leo Forbstein. Songs: "I Want What I Want When I Want It," "Kiss Me Again," "Mascot of the Troops" and "The Time, The Place and The Girl," music by Victor Herbert, lyrics by Henry M. Blossom. Cast: Walter Pidgeon, Bernice Claire, Edward Everett Horton, June Collyer, Frank McHugh, Claude Gillingwater, Judith Voselli, Albert Gran, Eleanor Gutchrlein, Karla Gutchrlein, Gino Corrado, Lionel Belmore, George Davis. Original Titles: *Mlle. Modiste*; *The Toast of the Legion*. *Mademoiselle Modiste* was filmed by First National in 1926, but not with a Foreign Legion setting.

New York Times, January 8, 1931: "...a most satisfactory entertainment. It has enough story to keep one interested..."

Synopsis: A general wishes his daughter to marry a legionnaire, but she loves another soldier. The legionnaire her father wants her to marry is also in love with another woman, a fashion model, who is hoping to be a great singer. One day the legionnaire overhears the two planning to elope. He learns the woman's address and goes to see her, offering her money not to marry the soldier. She initially refuses, but when the soldier's father explains that his son will be ostracized if he marries her. She then agrees not to marry him unless asked by his father himself. Using an assumed name, she gets a job as a cabaret singer. The legionnaire is unable to locate her before his regiment is sent to Algiers. Meanwhile, she becomes an opera singer and is unwittingly hired by the soldier's father to sing at the party celebrating his regiment's return. The soldier is glad to see her, although his father still expects him to marry the other woman, who is planning her elopement with the man she loves. The legionnaire vows he will marry the singer despite his father's objections. Pleased to see his son taking a stand, the father agrees to let him marry the singer.

Kiss Me Again (First National, 1931) Walter Pidgeon, Bernice Claire

THE RED SHADOW

Vitaphone/Warner Bros. Released December 3, 1932. 2 reels. Broadway Brevities No. 7. Director: Roy Mack. Photography: E. B. DuPar. Story: Jack Henley and Cleo Lambert, based on the operetta *The Desert Song* by Lawrence Schwab, Otto Harbach, Oscar Hammerstein II, Sigmund Romberg and Frank Mandel. Cast: Alexander Gray, Bernice Claire, Max Stamm, Grace Worth, Ahi, G. Yourlo, Reginald Carrington, the Lester Cole Ensemble.

Synopsis: The son of a Legion general is a wastrel and an embarrassment to his father. The commander of a Legion fort in Morocco suggests that the son be enlisted in the French Foreign Legion to make a man of him, to which the general agrees. One year later, the Legion is being harassed by the Red Shadow and his band. The Red Shadow is really the general's son, but no one other than a native dancing girl knows. When the Red Shadow is caught, he is challenged to a duel by the general but refuses to fight him. Puzzled, the general then learns the Red Shadow's true identity from the dancing girl.

Filmed at the Vitaphone studio in Brooklyn, New York. Stock footage from the 1929 *The Desert Song* was utilized in the outdoor scenes. Another short with the same title was released by Universal in early 1932 as "A Shadow Detective Mystery" and based on the story *The Red Scare* by Ronald Everson.

SHEIK TO SHEIK

Warner Bros. Released October 10, 1936. 22mins. Broadway Brevities. Director: Roy Mack. Story: A. Dorian Olvos, Cyrus Wood. Cinematography: Ray Foster. Editor: Bert Frank. Music: Mann Curtis, Sanford Green and Cliff Hess. Musical Director: David Mendoza. Dance Arranger: Harland Dixon. Cast: Georges Metaxa, Ann Barrie, John Berkes, The Buccaneers, Elsa, Marley, Richard Rober.

THE DESERT SONG

Warner Bros. Released January 29, 1944. 96mins. Technicolor. Director: Robert Florey. Producer: Robert Buckner. Photography: Bert Glennon. Screenplay: Robert Florey, Robert Buckner, based upon a play by Lawrence Schwab, Otto Harbach, Oscar Hammerstein II, Sigmund Romberg and Frank Mandel. Art Director: Charles Novi. Editor: Frank Magee. Makeup: Perc Westmore. Gowns: Milo Anderson. Dialogue Director: Harold Winston. Music Adaptation: H. Roemheld. Additional Song: Gay Parisienne by Jack Scholl and Serge Walter. Dance Numbers Staged/Directed: LeRoy Prinz. Special Effects Director: Lawrence Butler. Special Effects: Edwin B. DuPar. Set Decorator: Jack McConaghy. Asst. Director: Art Lueker. Cast: Dennis Morgan, Irene Manning, Bruce Cabot, Lynne Overman, Gene Lockhart, Faye Emerson, Victor Francen, Curt Bois, Jack La Rue, Marcel Dalio, Nestor Paiva, Gerald Mohr, Felix Basch, Noble Johnson, Wallis Clark, Fritz Leiber, George Renavent, William Edmunds, Egon Brecher, Duncan Renaldo, Albert Morin, George Dobbs, Paul Bryar, Franco Corsaro, Francis McDonald, Joseph Crehan, George Sorel, Anthony Warde, Frank Arnold, Louis Mercier.

The Exhibitor, December 29, 1943: "This stage hit has been faithfully transferred to the screen, but with touches of the modern added....the adventure sequences...contain action, suspense, novel settings, and a touch of freshness."

Variety, December 15, 1943: "Despite modernization to provide film technique and movement to the operetta, basic entertainment qualities of 'The Desert Song' are retained to provide most diverting audience reaction..."

Synopsis: This version opens in Geneva in 1939 at a meeting of contractors from several different nations bidding to build a railroad in Morocco. In that North African country, a native tribe called Riffs is being led by a Frenchman calling himself El Khobar. They are attempting to halt construction of the railroad because a local sheik is in favor of it and has coerced the Legion into fighting the Riffs. The Frenchman doubles as a nightclub pianist so as to be able to gather inside information on what the Legion is planning. He also gets a female cabaret singer to help him. When he captures one of the sheik's minions, El Khobar offers to swap him for Riffs being held prisoner by the sheik; the latter agrees. El Khobar then meets with some Riff leaders to get them to treaty for peace with France if the French order the sheik out of Morocco. Before they can, legionnaires attack the main Riff village. When the Riffs try to flee, they are surrounded, although El Khobar manages to escape. The singer inadvertently reveals El Khobar's secret identity to a Legion officer. The pianist informs the officer that the Germans are the ones to benefit from the railroad and together they steal some papers from the sheik's office as proof of this. They are caught and in the ensuing fight, the officer kills the sheik. The officer then goes to Paris with the papers. As a result, the Riffs are given fair treatment and work on the railroad proceeds under the auspices of the French government.

This version was filmed in 72 days from June to September 1942, at a cost of $107,000. This was Robert Florey's (1900-1979) final film under his Warner Bros. contract and his sole picture made in color. Censorship problems occurred with scenes of legionnaires abusing Arabs, resulting in cuts. This remake differs from the others by altering the plot to fit the current world situation. The character of "The Red Shadow" became "El Khobar." Location shooting included a Native American reservation near Gallup, New Mexico.

THE DESERT SONG

Warner Bros. Released May 30, 1953. 110mins. Technicolor. Director: Bruce Humberstone. Writer: Roland Kibbee, based upon a play by Sigmund Romberg, Laurence Schwab, Oscar Hammerstein II, Frank Mandel and Otto Harbach. Photography: Robert Burks. Art Direction: Stanley Fleischer. Music Adaptation: Max Steiner. Editor: William Ziegler, A.C.E. Orchestrations: Murray Cutter. Wardrobe: Leah Rhodes, Marjorie Best. Producer: Rudi Fehr. Set Decorator: William L. Kuehl. Makeup: Gordon Bau. Musical Direction: Ray Heindorf. Musical Numbers Staged/Directed: Leroy Prinz. Assistant Director: Russell Saunders. Technical Advisor: Dru Hatswell. Song "Gay Parisienne" by Jack Scholl and Serge Walter. Cast: Kathryn Grayson, Gordon MacRae, Steve Cochran, Raymond Massey, Dick Wesson, Allyn McLerie, Ray Collins, Paul Picerni, Frank DeKova, William Conrad, Trevor Bardette, Mark Dana.

Motion Picture Exhibitor, May 6, 1953: "...adventure, intrigue, and romance, good performances, and adequate direction and production...better than average package box office-wise."

New York Times, May 21, 1953: "...a handsome, burnished Technicolor backdrop to Sigmund Romberg's sandy rhapsodies, which...never sounded prettier....Bruce Humberstone's bumbling direction merely underlines the pedantic dialogue, as does the generally indifferent emoting."

Synopsis: A Frenchman named Paul Bernard moonlights as a leader of the Riff tribe in Morocco, where he is known as "El Khobar." Believed by the French to be their enemy, he actually is aiding the Riffs so that they will not attack the French. He is thwarted by a local Arab sheik who is playing the French against the Riffs until he is strong enough to attack the French. Bernard thus finds himself caught between the two. As Bernard, he is an anthropologist and professor, and is asked by a visiting French general to tutor his capricious daughter who has come to Morocco out of boredom with school in France. He falls for the beautiful daughter as Bernard, but she is not interested in him. Later, while strolling through a garden at night, she meets El Khobar and becomes attracted to him. Meanwhile, the Arab sheik has captured some Legion machine guns and is planning to attack their fort. A dancing girl named Azuri learns of this and informs El Khobar, with whom she is in love. He, meanwhile, meets the general's daughter and pleads his case, but she doesn't believe him and informs a Legion officer of his presence in the fort. El Khobar eludes him and kidnaps the daughter. The sheik learns of this and sends men to grab the daughter from the Riff camp, figuring the general will be grateful to him for having done so. The Riffs attack the sheik's palace and are aided by a patrol of legionnaires. The sheik's true intentions revealed, he is taken away. Bernard emerges from the palace holding his El Khobar disguise and informs the general that the Riff leader is dead. The daughter is crushed at the news, but later Bernard appears in a garden where the daughter is and sings to her as El Khobar had earlier, and she sings back, and presumably they live happily in tune ever after.

The Desert Song (Warner Bros., 1953) Lobby card

The Desert Song (Warner Bros., 1953) Kathryn Grayson, Gordon MacRae

CHAPTER SIX
Shifting Sands: Films of the Post-World War II Legion

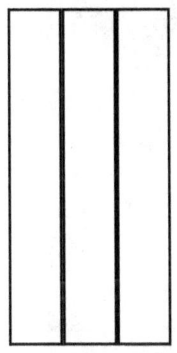

World War II was the cause of wholesale changes on the planet. Pessimism and realism almost totally replaced romanticism and advances in technology were reflected in every genre of film. Foreign Legion films kept in step for the most part, noting the changes in the area of uniforms, politics and technology. In the early 1950s, beginning with French Indo-China, France began losing her colonies, which eventually led to less of a need for the Foreign Legion and a reduction in its size.

Filmography

ROGUES' REGIMENT

Universal-International. Released November 16, 1948. 86mins. Director: Robert Florey. Writer: Robert Buckner. Producer: Robert Buckner. Photography: Maury Gertsman, A.S.C. Music: Daniele Amfitheatrof, David Tomkin, Milton Schwarzwald. Editor: Ralph Dawson. Art Directors: Bernard Herzbrun, Gabriel Scognamillo. Dance Direction: Billy Daniel. Set Decoration: Russell A. Gausman, Oliver Emery. Technical Advisor: Paul Coze. Makeup: Bud Westmore. Hair Stylist: Carmen Dirigo. Asst. Director: Horace Hough. Miss Toren's Gowns: Orry-Kelly. Miss Toren's Songs: Jack Brooks and Serge Walter--"Just for Awhile," "Who Can Tell." Music Supervisor: Milton Schwarzwald. Orchestrations: David Tomkin. Cast: Dick Powell, Vincent Price, Marta Toren, Stephen McNally, Edgar Barrier, Carol Thurston, Richard Loo, Philip Ahn, Frank Conroy, James Millican, Henry Rowland, Richard Fraser, Otto Reichow, Kenny Washington, Dennis Dongate, Martin Garralaga, James F. Nolan, Paul Bryar, Gordon Clark, Lester Sharpe, Eugene Borden, Maurice Marsac, Victor Sen Yung, John Doucette, Ken Harvey.

Rogues' Regiment (Universal-International, 1948) Dick Powell, Philip Ahn

The Exhibitor, October 13, 1948: "Containing a goodly portion of action and suspense as well as the saleable French Foreign Legion angle…"

Variety, October 6, 1948: "Writing is not too imaginative, but…integrates all of the standard tricks…to keep the pic on the move and reasonably exciting."

Harrison's Reports, October 2, 1948: "The story and treatment follow a familiar pattern….it moves along at a pretty fast pace and has considerable excitement…"

Synopsis: A top-ranking Nazi, who had ordered a Sgt. Rowland to burn the bodies of Adolf Hitler and Eva Braun in 1945, later joins the Foreign Legion in French Indochina as a former German private, Carl Reicher. On a train bound for Saigon, a Dutch art and antique dealer named Van Ratten has his servant kill French Colonel Lemercier, who knows that he is really a German involved in smuggling Russian guns. Van Ratten, knowing Reicher to be a former SS officer, sends him to an Arab to have his Nazi tattoo removed. This done, Reicher kills the Arab. At the café *Petite Tonkinoise,* singer Lili Maubert is really a French agent. She is contacted by Whit Corbett of U.S. Army Intelligence, who is assigned to capture Reicher who has never been photographed. A Legion patrol is attacked by Vietnamese rebel Tran Duy Gian; Reicher shoots Rowland, who is also a legionnaire, in the back to silence him, but before he dies, Rowland reveals Reicher's identity to Corbett. Reicher escapes, killing Van Ratten in the process, because he wanted to be overpaid for securing a passport, then kills the dealer's servant. Corbett captures him; he is hanged after the Nuremberg trials, and Corbett and Lili marry.

Shifting Sands: Films of the Post-World War II Legion

This film was banned in France and all French possessions due to its disrespectful depiction of the Legion. The character of Reicher was based on top Nazi Martin Bormann, who was still at large at the time. This was the last feature film both directed and written by Robert Florey, and his final collaboration with writer Robert Buckner (1906-1989). The latter got his idea for the scenario from a *Life* magazine article dealing with the infiltration of the post-war French Foreign Legion by German Nazis. With a budget of about $1.13 million, *Rogues Regiment* took about six weeks to make.

OUTPOST IN MOROCCO

Moroccan Pictures/United Artists. Released May 2, 1949. 92mins. Director: Robert Florey. Executive Producer: Samuel Bischoff. Story: Joseph N. Ermolieff. Screenplay: Charles Grayson and Paul de Sainte Colombe. Director of Photography: Lucien Andriot. Producer: Paul N. Ermolieff. Art Director: Arthur Lonergan. Editor: George Arthur. Musical Score: Michel Michelet. Set Decorator: Robert Priestley. Production Supervisor: Ben Hersh. Makeup: Mel Berns. Asst. Director: Joe Depew. Hair Stylist: Ann Locker. Cast: George Raft, Marie Windsor, Akim Tamiroff, John Litel, Eduard Franz, Erno Verebes, Crane Whitley, Damian O'Flynn, Michael Ansara.

Harrison's Reports, March 26, 1949: "...a routine, well-dressed action feature....an ineffective rehash of the plots that have been used in many other Legion films...."

The Exhibitor, March 30, 1949: "...it makes for generally interesting entertainment, with the cast capable."

Synopsis: A Legion officer becomes involved with the daughter of a local sheik when he escorts her home after her return from Europe. The sheik is planning a revolt against the French. The Legion learns this after recovering proof of new rifles being smuggled to local tribesmen. A detail of Legion volunteers attempts to destroy the sheik's arsenal, but are too late. The sheik, meanwhile, wipes out a fort near his city. The officer's detachment rebuilds part of the fort and holds the daughter hostage, but she is let go by the officer when it appears their water will run out completely. The next day a rainstorm occurs and the mud walls collapse. The detachment plants mines in the area around the fort and await the attack they know will come. When no other tribes appear, the sheik decides to attack only with his own force. His daughter attempts to stop him, but arrives as the attack is beginning. She rides along with his force trying to reach her father, but is killed when the mines are exploded. The attack is beaten off, and later the other tribes appear and renew their allegiance to the French.

This film includes footage shot in Morocco of actual legionnaires. It was made in just 36 days during August and September of 1948.

JUMP INTO HELL

Warner Bros. Released May 14, 1955. 92mins. Director: David Butler. Producer: David Weisbart. Screenplay: Irving Wallace. Photography: J. Peverell Marley. Editor: Irene Morra. Music: David Buttolph. Cast: Jack Sernas, Kurt Kasznar, Arnold Moss, Peter Van Eyck,

Marcel Dalio, Norman Dupont, Lawrence Dobkin, Pat Blake, Irene Montwill, Alberto Morin, Maurice Marsac, Louis Mercier.

Variety, March 30, 1955: "...the viewer is never caught up in what's transpiring on the screen....The human problems posed and the dialog...are strictly formula."

Motion Picture Exhibitor, April 6, 1955: "As an attempt at recreating the conditions and brutality of the Dienbienphu fighting the film is highly successful. An air of authenticity surrounds the production, resulting in a well-paced and exciting entry."

Synopsis: Four Foreign Legion officers are recruited to reinforce a besieged fortress at Dienbienphu in Indochina. They parachute in only to find that the enemy has closed all escape routes. Ordered to fight to the death by the fort commandant, two of them manage to get away with dispatches before the fort is taken.

DESERT OUTPOST

C.G.A./Anglo-Amalgamated (U.S./France). Released 1955. 67mins. Directors: Sam Newfield, Marcel Cravenne. Photography: Louis Page. Music: Guy Luypaetrz. Producer: Serge Glykson. Cast: Buster Crabbe, Fuzzy Knight, Cullen Crabbe, Gilles Queant, Jacqueline Porel, Francine Brandt, Pascale Roberts.

Synopsis: Capt. Gallant uncovers a plot to assassinate a visiting general. He next comes to the assistance of one of his men who has fallen in love with an Arab dancing girl and is suspected of murdering an influential business man, a rival for her affections. The real murderer is discovered by Capt. Gallant. Later, Gallant and his men are ambushed by the forces of a formerly friendly sheik. He discovers that the sheik and his daughter are being held prisoners by an unscrupulous renegade, whom Gallant proceeds to outwit.

This is a compilation of three episodes of the TV series *Captain Gallant*. (See Chapter Nine.)

DESERT SANDS

Bel-Air/United Artists. Released September 1956. 87mins. Technicolor. Director: Lesley Selander. Producer: Howard W. Koch. Screenplay: George W. George, George F. Slavin and Danny Arnold, from the novel *Punitive Action* by John Robb. Photography: Gordon Avril. Editor: John F. Schryer. Special Photographic Effects: Howard A. Anderson. Music: Paul Dunlap. Cast: Ralph Meeker, Marla English, J. Carrol Naish, John Smith, Ron Randell, Keith Larsen, John Carradine, Jarl Victor, Lita Milan, Otto Waldis, Peter Mamakos, Albert Carrier.

Harrison's Reports, August 13, 1955: "'Desert Sands' offers enough excitement and suspense to satisfy the undiscriminating action devotees, even though the story is run-of-the-mill and has been given an unimaginative treatment."

New York Times, November 19, 1955: "Lesley Selander directed...for a maximum of gun smoke and a minimum of reasonableness and competence."

Shifting Sands: Films of the Post-World War II Legion

Synopsis: The brother of an Arab chieftain has him assassinated by men disguised as Foreign Legionnaires; his young son and daughter vow vengeance against the French. Fifteen years later the grown children begin their revenge, first wiping out a relief column on its way to an outpost, then taking the fort itself. The new commanding officer at the post turns out to be an old acquaintance, so the son gives him a chance to save his remaining men by agreeing to set a trap for the next relief force which is already on its way. The officer and daughter fall in love, complicating things. As the hidden Arabs wait for the relief force to enter the fort, the daughter frees the officer and he is able to save his men from being massacred in a hard-fought battle. The officer kills the leader as he is about to kill his sister, and she is promised leniency at her trial.

Desert Sands (Bel-Air/United Artists, 1956) **Lobby card**

CHINA GATE

20th Century-Fox. Released May 22, 1957. 90mins. Director/Producer/Writer: Samuel Fuller. Photography: Joseph Biroc. Music: Victor Young and Max Steiner. Editor: Gene Fowler, Jr. Songs: Harold Adamson. Cast: Gene Barry, Angie Dickinson, Nat "King" Cole, Paul Dubov, Lee Van Cleef, George Givot, Gerald Milton, Neyle Morrow, Marcel Dalio, Maurice Marsac, Warren Hsieh, Paul Busch, Sasha Hardin, James Hong, William Soo Hoo.

China Gate (20th Century-Fox, 1957) Magazine ad

Shifting Sands: Films of the Post-World War II Legion

Motion Picture Exhibitor, May 15, 1957: "...a good deal of suspense and action... Performances are average, as is the direction and production."

Variety, May 22, 1957: "...is an over-long but sometimes exciting story of the battle between Vietnamese and Red Chinese, told through the efforts of a small band of French Foreign legionnaires... A novel touch is inserted through the dominating character being a beautiful Eurasian woman, who leads the Legion demolition patrol to its objective through enemy territory."

Synopsis: In 1954 a Vietnamese village holds its own against invading Red Chinese. They cannot win, though, unless the enemy's large ammo dump can be found and destroyed. A unit of French Foreign Legionnaires is led by a Eurasian woman who is known to the invaders. She asks only for asylum in the U.S. as her payment. She changes her mind when she learns that one of the men is the father of her child, who deserted her when the boy was born because of his Asian features. She again agrees to lead the unit, however, and a reconciliation between her and the man fails because he still refuses to accept the child. She locates the dump, but when the explosives fail to go off, she runs into the tunnel and sets them off, sacrificing her life. Her former lover and another legionnaire get away in a stolen plane and the lover is reunited with his son, with whom he returns home.

DESERT HELL

20th Century-Fox. Released June 25, 1958. 82mins. RegalScope. Director: Charles Marquis Warren. Producer: Robert W. Stabler. Screenplay: Endre Bohem, from a story by C. M. Warren. Photography: John M. Nicholaus, Jr. Music: Raoul Kraushaar. Production Manager/Asst. Director: Nathan R. Barragar. Editor: Fred W. Berger. Art Direction: James W. Sullivan. Set Decoration: Raymond Boltz, Jr. Sound: Jack Goodrich. Wardrobe: Byron Munson. Makeup: Jack Dusick. Special Photographic Effects: Jack Rabin and Louis DeWitt. Cast: Brian Keith, Barbara Hale, Richard Denning, John Desmond, Philip Pine, Richard Shannon, Duane Grey, Charles Gray, Lud Veigel, Richard Gilden, Ronald Foster, John Verros, Patrick O'Moore, Bill Hamel, Roger Etienne, Felix Locher, Michael Pate, Ben Wright, Albert Carrier, Boghwan Singh.

Variety, June 18, 1958: "Routine meller...well photographed. Cast gives a good account of itself."

Motion Picture Exhibitor, June 25, 1958: "It is a weary and time-consuming yarn that is loaded with talk, talk, and more talk. ... The cast is adequate and the direction and production standard."

Synopsis: After a Legion patrol is ambushed by Tauregs, only two legionnaires survive. The pair, a captain and a sergeant, are given a new patrol and ordered to warn all the Legion outposts of the Taureg uprising. Before they depart, the captain finds his wife in the arms of one of his men, a lieutenant. The patrol comes under constant attack as it marches toward the first outpost, losing many men. The captain learns that although the Taureg chieftain is signing a peace treaty at the outpost, a faction of his tribe is planning to assassinate him and blame it on the French, thus inciting a new war. The patrol manages to warn the Taureg leader, but both the captain and lieutenant are mortally wounded. Before he dies, the lieutenant assures the captain of his wife's fidelity.

Desert Hell (20th Century-Fox, 1958) Lobby card

LEGION OF THE DOOMED

Allied Artists-Wm. F. Broidy Pictures Corp. Released March 12, 1958. 75mins. Director: Thor Brooks. Writers: Tom Hubbard and Fred Eggers. Photography: John J. Martin, A.S.C. Editor: Herbert R. Hoffman. Art Director: Erwin Yessin. Asst. Director: Ralph Slosser. Set Decorator: Pat Delaney. Dialogue Supervisor: David Bond. Set Continuity: Eleanor Donahoe. Property Master: Arthur Wasson. Wardrobe: Mike Harte. Makeup: Ted Coodley. Producer: William F. Broidy. Associate Producer: Erwin Yessin. Recording: Ralph Butler. Cast: Bill Williams, Dawn Richard, Anthony Caruso, Kurt Kreuger, Tom Hubbard, John Damler, Rush Williams, George Baxter, Saul Gorss, Joseph Abdullah, Hal Gerard, Richard Farnsworth, Zeev Bufman, Rick Vallin, Gary Kent, Spiros Casimas, Yvonne deLavallade, Bud Wolfe, Vicki Bakkan, Darlene Fields.

New York Times, March 12, 1959: "...a dreadful little drama...The only...asset is some occasional hard-bitten trouping by Bill Williams, as a stalwart legionnaire...."

Subtitled Sands: Foreign Foreign Legion Films

Synopsis: An American in the Foreign Legion, Lt. Smith, is serving in Algeria under the tyrannical command of Capt. Marcheck. Marcheck is plotting with his native clerk, Karaba, to turn against the French and form an alliance with the Berbers. He assigns Smith to take a patrol from their remote outpost and report to Col. Lesperance at Sidi-Bel-Abbes. Marcheck plots with the natives to ambush the patrol, but Smith and his men fight them off. At night in Sidi-Bel-Abbes, Smith is attacked by a native chief and another assassin but escapes by running into the room of Dalbert Marcheck, who wants to find her husband so he will sign French divorce papers. Unaware of her identity, Smith falls in love with Dalbert. Next morning, however, Col. Lesperance orders Smith to let Dalbert join his patrol so she can visit her husband at the outpost. The party is also joined by Brodie, a correspondent writing stories about the Legion. When they reach the outpost, Marcheck refuses the divorce and continues with his plans against the French. He weakens the garrison by sending a strong detachment to another fort, where they are almost immediately ambushed and wiped out. Marcheck wears down his remaining force by sending the men on almost continuous twenty-four-hour desert patrols, despite Smith's protests. Brodie, however, forces the hands of Marcheck and Karaba when he recognizes the native as a noted Arab leader. He passes the word to Smith, but Karaba overhears their conversation. He and Marcheck overpower Smith, but in a game of wits Smith goads Karaba into killing Marcheck. There is a terrific fight but Karaba escapes into the desert and organizes his Berbers for an all-out attack on the garrison. Smith, however, marches his men into the desert to attack the Berber ammunition dump. There is a fearful battle and against tremendous odds the Legionnaires slaughter the Berbers. Karaba is killed and Smith returns to Dalbert.

Legion of the Doomed (Allied Artists/Wm. F, Broidy Pictures, 1958)
Bill Williams, Dawn Richard

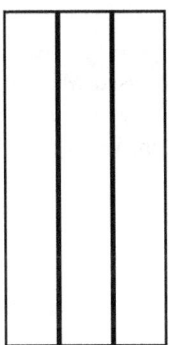

CHAPTER SEVEN
Subtitled Sands: Foreign Foreign Legion Films

With the actual French Foreign Legion having fought in all corners of the globe, it is only natural that films about the corps should have been made in a number of countries, certainly in France at the very least. The truth is that several countries in both Europe and North America as well as a couple in Asia have produced motion pictures featuring the famed fighting force. Many of them were released only in their country of origin, resulting in some scarce data. Release dates given are those for the country of origin except where noted.

Filmography

DIE FREMDENLEGION
(*THE FOREIGN LEGION*)
Continetal-Kunstfilm GmbH (Berlin, Germany). Released 1912.

LE LEGIONNAIRE
Le Film D'Art/Agence Generale de Cin'matographie (France). Released February 1914. 3 reels. Director: Henri Pouctal. Story: Yves Mirande. Scenario: H. Pouctal. Cast: Leon Mathot.

Le Journal, February 13, 1914: "With *Le Legionnaire* the intention of Le Film D'Art was to make us familiar with the little known and for many mysterious world of The Foreign Legion, which is an almost holy asylum where outcasts and lost souls of all countries come to bury their past. *Le Legionnaire* is not only a supremely moving picture for the dramatic action we witness but also because it was shot on location and reproduces real life scenes. It's an invaluable document of the highest interest, especially now that the Legion is so much talked about."

DIE FLUCHT AUS DER FREMDENLEGION
(FLIGHT FROM THE FOREIGN LEGION)
Continental Kunstfilm GmbH (Germany). Released April 1, 1916.

FREMDENLEGIONAR KIRSCH
(FOREIGN LEGIONNAIRE KIRSCH)
Bayerische Filmindustrie A. Ankenbrand GmbH (Munich, Germany). Released May 20, 1921. Director: Philipp Lothar Mayring. Part I--*Wie Ich in Die Legion Kam*. Part II--*In Der Legion*. Cast: Max Kirsch, Lisa Kresse, Philipp Lothar Mayring, Mario Sten, Joe Mathes, Benno Norbert, Max Bayerhammer, A. Nietra, Hans Hano.

LES FILS DU SOLEIL
(SONS OF THE SUN)
Societé des Cineromans/Pathé-Consortium-Cinema (France). Released November 19, 1924. 8 reels. Director: René le Somptier. Screenplay: Pierre Mercourt. Photography: Paul Guichard, Georges Lafont. Art Direction: Tony Lecain. Cast: Marquisette Bosky, Leila Djali, Georges Charlia, Joe Hamman, Marcel Vibert, Jean Bernier, Mario Nasthasio, César-Tullio Terrore, Geo Leclerc, Tahar Henache.

Eight Episodes:
1. *A Drama of Saint Cyr*
2. *Captain Youssouf*
3. *Christian and Muslim*
4. *The Justice of Abd el Kassem*
5. *Escape*
6. *Holy War*
7. *Sword Unsheathed*
8. *The Triumph of Honor.*

Synopsis: A ruthless Arab sheik, Abd el Kassem, rules over a region of Morocco, thanks to the weapons sold to him by Baron von Horn, an equally ruthless international financier. De Beauvoisin, a brilliant cadet of Saint-Cyr (the French equivalent of West Point), is forced to join the Legion after having been framed by von Horn who's in love with his fiancée Aurore. Aurore and her father are also forced to leave for Morocco, where the sheik becomes infatuated with her and abducts her. In the end, de Beauvoisin manages to free his fiancée, vanquish the sheik and punish von Horn.

DER FREMDENLEGIONAR
(THE FOREIGN LEGIONNAIRE)
Munchener Lichtspielkunst AG (Germany). Released March 1, 1928. 6 reels. Director: James Bauer. Screenplay: Max Ferner. Photography: Franz Koch. Music: Alexander Schirmann. Art Direction: Ludwig Reiber. Cast: Dorothea Wieck, Gustav Frohlich, Joop von Huken, Rio Nobile, Oscar Marion, Manfred Voss, Ferdinand Martini, Therese Giehse, Rolf Pinegger.

Fremdenlegionar Kirsch (B. F. A. Ankenbrand GmbH, 1921) Poster

DAS LETZTE FORT
(*THE LAST FORT*)
Nero-Film AG (Germany). Released November 24, 1928. 85mins. Director: Kurt Bernhardt. Producer: Gustav Schwab. Writers: Curt J. Braun, Marcel Hellman, Hermann Kosterlitz, Hans Wilhelm. Photography: Fritz Arno Wagner, Artur von Schwertfhrer. Art Direction: Julius von Borsody. Music: Hansheinrich Dransmann. Cast: Heinrich George, Alfred Gordel, Alexander Granach, Rolla Norman, Fritz Odemar, Maria Paudler, Albert Steinruck.

LE SERGENT X
Gloria Film/Osso (Germany/France). Released March 25, 1932. 91mins. Director: Vladimir Strijewski. Scenario: Ivan Loukasch. Photography: Nicolas Toporkoff. Art Directors: Ivan Lochakoff, Meingard. Music: René Mercier, Henri Forterre. Editor: Leonide Azar. Cast: Ivan Mousjoukine, Suzy Vernon, Bill Bocketts, Suzanne Stanley, Courtola, Nicole de Rouves, Jean Angelo, Leo Curtois, Michael Monda, Massazzo, Lars Birbach, Tinchtiaeff. Remade as *Sergent X* by Marceau (France) in 1960 [q.v.].

Variety, April 19, 1932: "…shows the spirit of the Foreign Legion…Good out of doors and spirit of North Africa vivid."

Synopsis: A Russian officer who is presumed dead joins the Foreign Legion. There, he meets the wife of a captain for the second time, but she does not recognize him. The captain is aware of the situation between them. The Russian keeps his distance, not wishing to upset their marriage.

INSULT
Paramount British (Great Britain). Released July 1932. 80mins. Director: Harry Lachman. Screenplay: Basil Mason, from a play by Jean Fabricus. Editor: David Lean. Cast: Elizabeth Allan, John Gielgud, Hugh Williams, Sam Livesey, Sydney Fairbrother, Abraham Sofaer, Edgar Norfolk, Hal Gordon, Dinah Gilly.

Synopsis: A half-caste legionnaire gives his life to save that of the governor, who is the son of a major who hates him.

DIE NACHT DER VERSUCHUNG
(*NIGHT OF TEMPTATION*)
(*FREMDENLEGIONAR NR. 37*)
Münchner Lichtspielkunst AG/Emelka (Germany). Released August 9, 1932. 71mins. Directors: Robert Wohlmuth, Leo Laszlo. Photography: Karl Hasselman. Music: Peter Kreuder, Friedrich Jung. Cast: Elga Brink, Werner Fuetterer, Lotte Deyers, Josef Eichheim, Walter Lantzsch, Otto Wernicke, Therese Giehse, Tono Forster-Larrinaga, Ludwig Ruppert, Max Schreck, Ernst Schlott, Ola Ocouma, Alexandre Mihalesco, Karl Raab.

The censors refused to let this film be released under its original title, *Fremdenlegionar Nr. 37 (Foreign Legionnaire No. 37)*, in June 1932 until the title was changed and certain cuts made.

GLOS PUSTYNI
(VOICE IN THE DESERT)

BMB Film (Poland). U.S. Dist.: Capitol Film Exchange. Released September 29, 1932. 78min. Director: Michal Waszynski. Screenplay: Eugeniusz Bodo, based on the novel *Sokol Pustyni* by Ferdynand Antoni Ossendowski. Photography: Seweryn Steinwurzel. Art Direction: Stefan Norris. Music: Henryk Wars. Production Managers: Witold Dybowski, Tadeusz Kallwejt. Cast: Nora Ney, Eugeniusz Bodo, Maria Bogda, Adam Brodzisz, Witold Conti, Janusz Dziewonski, Kazimierz Jarocki, Pawel Owerllo, Stefan Wroncki, Mieczyslaw Gielniewski.

Synopsis: A Polish adventurer is captured by an Algerian sheik. With the help of the sheik's wife he escapes and joins the Foreign Legion, which sends a force to overthrow the sheik.

LE GRAND JEU
(THE GREAT GAME)

Films de France/Pathé (France). Released May 2, 1934. 120mins. Director: Jacques Feyder. Story, Continuity and Dialogue: Jacques Feyder and Charles Spaak. Photography: Harry Stradling and Maurice Forster. Music: Hanns Eisler. Asst. Directors: Marcel Carne, Charles Barrois. Art Director: Lazare Meerson. Editor: Jacques Brillouin. Cast: Francoise Rosay, Pierre Richard-Willm, Georges Pitoeff, Camille Bert, Pierre de Guingand, Andre Dubosc, Pierre Larquey, Nestor Ariani, Marie Bell, Louis Florencie, Line Clevers, Olga Velbria, Charles Vanel, Maryse Wendling, Jacques Normand, Geno Ferny, Pierre Labry. Remade in 1954 by Cinedio/Dominant [q.v.].

Variety, May 15, 1934: "Emphasis is on the story...essentially one of the Legion...the atmosphere comes in right where it should...a drama with genuine and compelling human interest."

Synopsis: A young French businessman suffers financial ruin due to his lover's extravagances. He is forced to leave the country, so he joins the Foreign Legion, where he shares lodgings with a Russian. At a local bar he meets a prostitute and singer who is the double of his former lover. He becomes fascinated by her and they live together. When the Russian attacks the woman, the Frenchman kills him. The woman makes it look like an accident. When his enlistment is up, the Frenchman plans to return to France with the woman. When he meets his old flame in Casablanca on the eve of his departure, he learns that she is now the mistress of a wealthy Arab. He forgets about the new woman, tricking her into returning to France alone. He then reenlists in the Legion.

Le Grand Jeu (Films de France/Pathé, 1934) Poster

JUAREZ Y MAXIMILIANO
(U.S.: JUAREZ AND MAXIMILIAN)

Miguel Contreras Torres (Mexico). U.S. Dist.: Columbia (1935). Released June 28, 1934. 98min. Aka *La caida del imperio (The Fall of the Empire); Antorchas de libertad (Torches of Freedom)*. Directors: Miguel Contreras Torres and Raphael J. Sevilla. Screenplay: Miguel C. Torres. Cinematography: Ezequiel Carrasco, Ross Fisher, Manuel Gomez Urquiza, Arthur Martinelli, Alex Phillips. Original Music: James C. Bradford, Max Urban. Editor: José Marino. Production Design: José Rodriquez Granada, Mariano Rodriquez Granada, Ramon R. Granada. Costumes: Emma Roldan. Assistant Director: Miguel M. Delgado. Cast: Enrique Herrera, Medea de Novara, Fernando Nava Ferriz, Carlos Orellana, Matilde Palou, Carlos Lopez, Ramon Peon, Luis G. Barreiro, Emma Roldan, Mario Martinez Casado, Roberto E. Guzman, Jesus Melgarejo, Victorio Blanco, Julio Villarreal, Alberto Miquel, J. Enriquez, Alfredo del Diestro, Abraham Galan, Alberto Galan, Joaquin Busquets, A. Saenz, Antonio R. Frausto, Ricardo Carti, Maria Luisa Zea, Angel T. Sala, Manuel Tomes, Dolores Camarillo, Mario Martinez Casado, Froylan B. Tenes, Godofredo del Castillo.

Synopsis: An account of Maximilian's time in Mexico, from his arrival to his execution.

LOST IN THE LEGION

British International Pictures/Wardour (Great Britain). Released August 1934. 66min. Director: Fred Newmeyer. Story: Syd Courtenay, Lola Harvey. Screenplay: Syd Courtenay, John Paddy Carstairs. Photography: Jack Parker. Cast: Leslie Fuller, Renee Houston, Betty Fields, Hal Gordon, H. F. Maltby, Alf Goddard, James Knight, Mike Johnson, A. Bromley Davenport.

Synopsis: Two ship's cooks accidentally enlist in the Foreign Legion, where they end up rescuing two women from a harem.

UN DE LA LEGION
(ONE OF THE LEGION)

Productions Calamy (France). Released September 18, 1936. 91min. Director: Christian-Jaque. Scenario: Pierre Schild. Music: Mahieddine, Casimir Oberfeld. Dialogue: Paul Fekete. Photography: Fred Langenfeld, Charles Suin, André Germain. Editors: William Barrache, André Versein. Cast: Fernandel, Robert Le Vigan, Jacques Varennes, Paul Azais, Daniel Mendaille, Arthur Devere, Suzy Prim, Therese Dorny, Rolla Norman, Jean Kolb, Regine Danciurt, Paul Amiot, Georges Malkine, Eugene Stuber, Marcel Vidal.

Synopsis: A Canadian travels to Marseilles with his wife where she needs to go to claim an inheritance. While he waits for her, the man is approached by a Legion deserter, who gets him drunk and sends him to Sidi-Bel-Abbes as his replacement. There he is forced into the Foreign Legion and sent to Morocco.

Un De La Legion (Productions Calamy, 1936) Poster

SUBTITLED SANDS: FOREIGN FOREIGN LEGION FILMS

LES HOMMES SANS NOM
(*MEN WITHOUT A NAME*)
Votre Film (France). Released 1937. 94min. Director: Jean Vallée. Screenplay: J. Vallée, from the account by Jean Desvallieres. Photography: Georges Million, Boris Kaufman, Raymond Clunie. Music: Jane Bos. Production Design: Jean d'Eaubonne. Producer: A. Javet. Cast: Tania Fodor, Suzet Mais, Paulette Houry, Constant Remy, Thomy Bourdelle, Lucas Gridoux, Arthur Devere, Paul Escoffier, Lucien Galas, Robert Ozenne, Georges Poclet, Maurice Remy, Charles Redgie, Bertoux, A.S. Takal, Georges Torof, Georges Spanelly.

Synopsis: A fictionalized account of the life of Col. Henri de Corta, who was the brother-in-law of one Jean Desvallieres, a colonel on the Foreign Legion stationed in Morocco.

LEGIONS D'HONNEUR
(*LEGIONS OF HONOR*)
Societé du Film Legion d'honneur (France). Released 1938. 103mins. Director: Maurice Gleize. Writer: Jean Jose Frappa, from the story *La Griffe* (*The Claw*) by Jean Makis. Photography: Christian Matras. Music: Henri Tomaso. Cast: Charles Vanel, Abel Jacquin, Marie Bell, Pierre Renoir, Jacques Baumer, Camille Bert, Pierre Magnier, Jean Perier, Jim Gerald, Georges Prieur, Tony Murcie, Maurice Schultz, Milly Mathis.

Synopsis: A three-part story about a Legion officer who is court-martialed and dismissed from the Legion.

DIE FRAU UND DER TOD/VISION LOINTAINE
(*THE WOMAN AND DEATH/FAR AWAY VISION*)
Eoscop Film Ag (Basel and Berlin) (Switzerland-Germany). Released March 18, 1938. 101mins. Director: Leo Lapaire. Screenplay: L. Lapaire. Photography: Eduard Hoesch. Music: Wolfgang Russ-Bovelino. Editor: Else Baum. Producers: Josef A. Vesely and Robert Reubi. Cast: Katharina Merker, Karl Dannemann, Rudolf Klein-Rogge, Herman Gallinger, Lucie Fuchs, Max Knapp, Paula Ottzenn, Willi Ackermann, Herbert Baerlocher, Charles Ferdinand Vaucher, Kurt Blanckharts, Bob Engel, Wilkins Taylor, Kandou, Heddy Bert, Fritz Obitsch, Max Dora. Original title: *Abenteurer in Marokko* (*Adventure in Morocco*).

LA GRANDE INCONNUE
(*THE GREAT UNKNOWN ONE*)
R.A.C. Dist. (France). Released May 5, 1939. Director: Jean d' Esme. Cast: Charles Denin, Oreste Gibilini. Documentary.

LE CHEMIN DE L'HONNEUR
(*THE PATH OF HONOR*)
Les Productions H. Garat (France). Released 1939. 105mins. Director: Jean-Paul Paulin. Screenplay: Jan Rentes. Photography: René Guissart, René Colas. Music: Georges Van Parys. Editor: Nic. Production Design: Lucien Aguettand, Marcel Magniez. Production Director: Robert Amsler. Cast: Renée Saint-Cyr, Marcelle Geniat, Jeanne Fusier-Gir, Mady Berry, Henri Garat, René Bergeron, Constant Remy, André Lefaur, Fernard Charpin, Lucas

Gridoux, Pierre Brasseur, Roland Toutain, Philippe Richard, Edy Depray, Georges Paulais, Paul Escoffier, Louis Allibert, Jean Poc, Marcel Chabrier.

This was dedicated to the memory of Roelof Revenues, a Dutch legionnaire using a French name, who was killed in battle in 1933.

FACE AU DESTIN
(FACING FATE)

Diffusions Intellectuelles (France). Released 1939. 84mins. Director: Henri Fescourt. Screenplay: Jean Desvallieres, based on a novel by Charles-Robert Dumas. Adaptation: Alfred Machard. Photography: Henri Barreyre, Marcel Villet. Production Design: Claude Bouxin. Music: Jean Lenoir, Mahieddine. Editor: Pierromax. Cast: Gaby Sylvia, Josselyne Gael, Marguerite Pierry, Mittyl Francia, Renée Morin, Ginette Cholsy, Reyna Capello, Yvonne Yma, Yvonne Rozille, Reine Mathicet, Josette France, Renée Veller, Blanche Denege, Monique Dantis, Paulette Berger, Georges Rigaud, Jules Berry, Jean Max, Jean Acquistapace, Jacques Gretillat, Francois Rozet, Robert Pizani, Henri Echourin, Rolla Norman, Paul Escoffier, Edy Debray, André Numes, Alfred Machard, Paul Boissin.

BETHSABEE

Compagnie Industrielle et Commercial Cinematigraphique (France). Released November 21, 1947. 97mins. Director: Leonide Moguy. Screenplay: Jacques Remy, Pierre Benoit, based on Benoit's novel. Cinematography: Nicholas Hyer. Music: Joseph Kosma. Producer: Raymond Bordecie. Cast: Danielle Darrieux, Georges Marchal, Jean Murat, Pierre-Louis, Olivier Darrieux, France Mooréa, Nicholas Vogel, Larbi Tounsi, Robert Daréne, André Clement, Paola Manelli, Mireille Ogy.

FORT DE LA SOLITUDE

UGCe Tamara Films (France). Released February 13, 1948. 90mins. Director: Robert Vernay. Screenplay: Bernard Zimmer, from the novel by René Guillot. Photography: Maurice Barry. Production Design: René Renoux, Raymond Gabutti. Music: Mohamed Yguerbouchen. Editor: Marthe Poncin. Cast: Claudine Dupuis, France Moorea, Made Siame, Paul Bernard, Alexandre Rignault, Lucien Nat, Michel Marsay, Jean-Jacques Delbo, Antoine Balpetre, Henri Couttet, Georges Hubert, Marcel Lupovici Robert Moncade, Paul Faivre, Leonce Corne, René Fluet, Albert Broquin, Robert le Flon, René Pascal, Riandreys.

HERMOSO IDEAL
(A WONDROUS IDEAL)

Ramex/RKO (Mexico). Released December 25, 1948. 80mins. Director: Alejandro Galindo. Screenplay: Gunther Gerzso. Adaptation: Salvador Novo and A. Galindo, from *Beau Ideal* by P.C. Wren. Photography: Jose Ortiz Ramos. Editor: Jorge Bustos. Music: Raul Lavista. Assistant Director: Moises M. Delgado. Head of Production: Antonio Guerrero Tello. Producer: J. M. Noriega. Song: "Callejuela Sin Salida" by Quintero Leon and Quiroga. Cast: Conchita Martinez, Rodolfo Landa, Changuerotti, Alejandro Cobo, Manuel Arvide, José Ortiz DeZurate, Lily Aclemar, Aurora Walker, José Baviera, Juan Calvo, Ramon Vallarino, Francisco Reiguera. Remake of *Beau Ideal* (1931) [q.v.]. Filmed at Estudios Churubusco.

Bethsabée (C. I. et C.C., 1947) Poster

Synopsis: Four Mexican children, Isabel, Pablo, Rafael and Luis (the latter two are brothers), make a pact to stay friends forever; Rafael and Isabel promise to marry. When Isabel tells the boys that her family is moving to Spain, Rafael promises to find her. Many years later in Spain, Rafael and Isabel are engaged when Rafael learns that Luis stole some important family papers. Rafael finds out that his brother ran off and joined the French Foreign Legion, so he vows to go and find him in order to restore the family honor. After he leaves, Pablo arrives in Spain and visits Isobel, bringing her the glove she had buried in Mexico when they were children. She had promised Rafael that she would wait for him, but confesses love for Pablo. She wants to be sure that Rafael's memory will not come between them, though. Pablo says he will find Rafael and bring him back so that Isabel may choose between them. Before he is able to enlist, Pablo learns that Rafael's brother was killed by an officer and that Rafael in turn killed the officer. For this he is sentenced to the penal battalion. Learning that to visit the penal battalion is impossible, Pablo asks another legionnaire how he can be sentenced to it. The legionnaire tells him that slapping an officer is a sure way. When the Legion plans to send some men from one fort to another, an officer and some men meet with some local sheiks to get their promise that they will not be attacked while on the march. The promise is given. While on the march, the officer loses his compass, the men run out of water and finally mutiny. A legionnaire shoots the officer, who picks Pablo as his replacement. Before he dies, a troop of Senegalese cavalry find the group; the officer tells their leader not to blame the men for the mutiny and points at Pablo just as he expires. The cavalry leader takes this to mean that Pablo was the leader of the mutiny; he and several others are court-martialed and sentenced to eight years in the penal battalion. There, another mutiny involving Pablo and Rafael breaks out; the two are placed in "the hole," along with several others as punishment. While there, the camp is attacked by Arabs and wiped out. The men in the hole have no food and die off until only Rafael and Pablo are left. The latter finally realizes that the other legionnaire is his long-lost friend when he uses a familiar term from their childhood. A passing group of Arabs rescues them, but takes them prisoner. Rafael is later returned to the Legion fort. Pablo escapes disguised as an Arab and heads for the fort just as the Arabs attack it. Pablo makes it safely into the fort and helps fight the Arabs, who are defeated when a large troop of Senegalese cavalry arrives. For their bravery, Pablo and Rafael are allowed any favor they wish. They quit the Legion and return to Spain and Isabel. She chooses Pablo for her husband.

Stock footage from *Beau Ideal* is evident in the battle scenes, and the same buildings were used for the Legion fort and Arab town.

AVEC LA RAFALE
(WITH A HAIL OF BULLETS)

(France). Released 1952. 14mins.

Synopsis: An armored train transports goods in a dangerous part of Indochina.

REGARDS SUR L'INDOCINE: NA-SAN UNE BATAILLE DANS LA JUNGLE
(A LOOK AT INDOCHINA: NA-SAN A BATTLE IN THE JUNGLE)

(France). Released 1952. 12mins. Producers: P. Lebon and Pierre Schoendorffer. Photography: George Kawai. Music: Tzipine.

LEGIONE STRANIERA
(FRANCE: LEGIONE ETRANGERE)
(UK: TROUBLE FOR THE REGIMENT)

Titanus/SocieteGenerale de Cinematograph (France/Italy). Released August 27, 1953. 90mins. Director: Basilio Franchina. Adaptation: A. de Stephani, Carlo Musso, B. Franchina. Photography: Mario Craveri. Music: Michele Cazzoli. Costumes: Dario Cecchi. Editor: Mario Serandrei. Production Design: Ottavio Scotti. Cast: Viviane Romance, Irene Galter, Alberto Farnese, Marc Lawrence, Enrico Olivieri, John Kitzmiller, Guido Celano, Enrico Glori, Giulio Cali, Turi Pandolfini, Bruno Smith, Antonio Gradoli, Emma Baron, Piero Pastore, Attilio Dottesio, Nando Di Claudio, Nino Vingelli, Corrado Nardi, Marcello Jannone, Leonello Zanchi, Maria Pia Bernardini, Sergio Crosia, Andrea Gallani, Anacleto Fasciuolo, Sandro Bianchi, Gino Anglani, Sylvie PelIayo, Ina La Yana.

Synopsis: Irene and Alberto plan to elope, but the girl misses the boat and a bitter Alberto arrives alone in Oran. He gets drunk and becomes infatuated with a nightclub singer named Cherie. He is accused of murder, but with Cherie's aid escapes from jail. He joins the Foreign Legion, where he is victimized by Sgt. Schwartz, Cherie's jealous lover. Irene and his brother Enrico go to his aid. The brothers meet at an outpost where the legionnaires are fighting Arabs. Enrico loses his life in an act of gallantry, and a wounded Alberto is reunited with Irene.

LE GRAND JEU
(U.S.: FLESH AND THE WOMAN)

Cinedio/Dominant (France/Italy). Released April 20, 1954. 102mins. Eastmancolor. Director: Robert Siodmak. Writer: Charles Spaak, based on *Le Grand Jeu* by Spaak and Jacques Feyder. Photography: Michel Kelber. Music: George Van Parys, Maurice Thiriet. Editor: V. Mercanton. Cast: Gina Lollobrigida, Jean-Claude Pascal, Arletty, Peter Van Eyck, Raymond Pellegrin, Jean Temerson, Jean Hebey, Leila Farida, Odette Barencey, Margo Lion, Lila Kedrova, Gabrielle Fontan, Alix Mahieu, Paul Amiot, Gerard Buhr. Remake of *Le Grand Jeu* (1934) [q.v.].

Synopsis: A Parisian lawyer falls in love with an Italian girl. They live together extravagantly; the man is caught practicing unethically and asked to resign from the bar. He goes to Algeria and tells the woman to sell their possessions and join him. She disobeys him and, broke and depressed, he joins the Foreign Legion, where he and two pals are sent to various posts for four years. Upon their return to Algeria, they go to a popular bar where the madam sets them up with three women. One of them is an exact double of the lawyer's former lover. The lawyer opts to get drunk and does not meet her; his two friends toss a coin for her.

SIDI-BEL-ABBES

Mapfilms/Cine Selections (France). Released April 30, 1954. 90mins. Color. Director: Jean-Alden Delos. Screenplay: J. Alden-Delos. Photography: Jean Isnard. Editor: André Brossier. Cast: Marc Valbel, Leila Farida, Marco Villa, Roland Toutain, Raymond Cordy, RobertTenton, Philippe Richard, Philippe Grey.

Le Grand Jeu (Cinedio/Dominant, 1954) Poster

SUBTITLED SANDS: FOREIGN FOREIGN LEGION FILMS

GELIEBTE FEINDIN
(BELOVED ENEMY)

Neue DeutscheFilmgesellschaft-Magna Film/Deutsche London Film (Germany). Released March 18, 1955. 98 mins. Director: Rolf Hansen. Screenplay: Jacob Geis and Juliana Kay, based on the novel by Maria von Kirchbach. Producers: Georg Richter, Conrad Flockner. Photography: Friedl Behn-Grund. Art Directors: Robert Herlth, Walter J. Blokesch. Sound: F. W. Dunstmann. Editor: Anna Hollering. Music: Mark Lothar. Cast: Werner Hinz, Ruth Leuwerik, Thomas Holtzmann, Wolf Dieter Maurer, Brigitte Stanzel, Rolf Henninger, Leonard Steckel, Gustav Knuth, Hans Quest, Otto Bruggemann, Wolf Ackva, Friedrich Domin, Hilda Weissner, Adolf Ziegler, Lina Carstens, Edith Schulze-Westrum, Kurt Stieler, Bruni Lobel, Margarete Henning-Roth, Walter Holten, Herbert Weicker, Erika Remberg.

LEJYON DONUSU
(BACK FROM THE FOREIGN LEGION)

Kazankaya Film (Turkey). Released 1957. 100mins. Director: Orhon Ariburnu. Writer: Safa Onal, from the novel by Hasan Kazankaya. Cinematography: Oren Turgud. Producer: H. Hazankaya. Cast: Fikret Hakan, Belgin Doruk, Arcay Muazzez, Ugur Basaran, Saime Bekbay, Cintay Asuman, Erbil Sadettin, Keptan Atif, Karan Sadri, Claudia Marc, Kadri Ogelman, Pervin Par, Halide Piskin, Salih Tozan, Nuri Genc, Kamran Yüce.

MADELEINE UND DER LEGIONAR
(MADELINE AND THE LEGIONNAIRE)
(U.S.: ESCAPE FROM SAHARA)

Melodie Film/UFA-Filmverleih (Germany). Released January 21, 1958. 101mins. Director: Wolfgang Staudte. Screenplay: Johannes Mario Simmel, Emil Burri and Werner Jorg Luddecke. Photography: Vaclav Vich. Asst. Director: Holger Lussmann. Editor: Martha Dübber. Music: Siegfried Franz. Costumes: Eva Maria Schroeder. Production Manager: Otto Meissner. Sound: Hans Lohmer. Cast: Hildegard Knef, Leonard Steckel, Friedrich Grass, Hannes Messemer, Werner Peters, Bernhard Wicki, Helmut Schmid, Joachim Hansen, Harry Meyer, Siegfried Lowitz, Hanita Hallan, Manfred Heidmann, Ursula Diestel, Horst Beck, Horst Beilke, Reinhold Bernt, Joachim Cadenbach, Ernst von Klipstein, Ursula Krieg, Tilly Lauenstein, Georg Lehn, Ludwig Linkers, Sigurd Lohde, Ralph Lothar, Friedrich Maurer, Oscar Sabo, Harold Sawade, Friedrich Schoenfelder, Karl Friedrich Schubert, Arthur Schroder, Herbert Stass, Walter Terrach, Horst Uhse, Carl Voscherau.

LOS LEGIONARIOS
(THE LEGIONNAIRES)

Producciones Zacarias (Mexico). Released August 7, 1958. 96mins. Director: Augustin P. Delgado. Story: Roberto Gomez Bolanos. Adaptation: R. H. Bolanos, A. P. Delgado. Photography: Alex Phillips. Production Design: Ramon Rodriguez Granada. Music: Manuel Esperon. Editor: Charles L. Kimball. Asst. Director: Moises M. Delgado. Cast: Maria Antonieta Pons, Marco Antonio Campos, Gaspar Henaine, Viruta y Capulina, Donna Behar, Luis Lomeli, Barbara Vicky Codina, Pedro de Aguillon, Manuel Vergara Manver, Marc Lambert.

SERGENT X

Marceau Productions (France). Released March 8, 1960. 95mins. Director: Bernard Borderle. Screenplay: Ivan Loukach, Jacques Robert, André Tabet. Photography: Claude Renoir. Editor: Christian Gaudin. Music: Georges Auric. Art Direction: René Moulaert. Producer: Ignace Morgenstern. Cast: Christian Marquand, Noelle Adam, Paul Guers, René Havard, Lutz Gabor, Daniel Cauchy, Renaud Mary, Moustache, Guy Mairesse, Veronique Verlhac, Yves Barsacq, Jean-Marie Riviére, Jacques Seller, Joelle Bernard, André Dumas, Paul Pavel, Jean Michaud. Remake of *Le Sergent X* (1932) [q.v.].

Sergent X **(Marceau Productions, 1960) Poster**

Subtitled Sands: Foreign Foreign Legion Films

Variety, March 16, 1960: "This remake, updated, of a pre-war actioner still seems old-fashioned. Outcome is foreshadowed and pace is plodding. Acting is ordinary with production and technical aspects good."

Synopsis: A paratrooper tries to drive a stolen truck and is injured in an accident. Prevented from returning home on schedule, his lover fears he has abandoned her. She then marries her boss. After his recovery, the man joins the Legion and has a fateful run-in with his former lover and her husband.

LEGIONNAIRE

(France). Released 1960. 20mins. Color. Director: Jacques Marcerou.

Synopsis: Documentary about the Legion and its retirement home in Puyloubier.

I DUE DELLA LEGIONE
(TWO LEGIONNAIRES)

Ultra Film/Titanus (Italy). Released August 16, 1962. 97mins. Director: Lucio Fulci. Screenplay: Antonio Leonviola, Roberto Bianchi Montero. Photography: Alfio Contini. Music: Luis Enriquez. Editor: Mario Serandrei. Cast: Franco Franchi, Ciccio Ingrassia, Rosalba Neri, Alighiero Noschese, Maria Teresa Vianello, Aldo Giuffre, Aldo Bufi Landi, Cesare Polacco, Nino Terzo, Jo Garso, Gianni Rizzo, Carlo Lombardi, Rosario Borelli, Gianni Crosio, Aldo Pini.

Synopsis: Two friends enlist in the Foreign Legion after having been wrongfully accused of murdering a gang boss.

MARCIA O CREPA
(MARCH OR DIE; aka THE LEGION'S LAST PATROL)
(U.S.: COMMANDO)

Tempo Film/Ficit/Galatea (Rome)/Midega (Madrid)/Monarchia-Zeyn Film (Munich)-Italy/Spain/West Germany/U.S. Dist.: Paramount. Released November 14, 1962. 104mins. Director: Frank Wisbar. Production Manager: Gabriela Silvestri. Story: Arturo Tofanelli. Screenplay: Giuseppe Mangione, Nino Guerrini, William Demby, Frank Wisbar, Enrico Bercovic. Photography: Cecilio Paniagua. Editor: Mario Serandrei. Music: Angelo Francesco Lavagnino. Art Director: Enrique Alarcon. Asst. Directors: Antonio N. Linares, Wieland Liebske. Sound: Luigi Puri. Cast: Stewart Granger, Dorian Gray, Maurizio Arena, Ivo Garrani, Fausto Tozzi, Riccardo Garrone, Carlos Casaravilla, Peter Carsten, Hans Von Borsody, Rafael Luis Calvo, Dietmar Schoenherr, Leo Anchoriz, Alfredo Mayo.

Synopsis: During the Algerian War in 1961, a Legion captain makes a daring raid to capture a rebel leader. The helicopter sent to retrieve them is shot down and the legionnaires and their prisoner are forced to make a cross-country journey. By the time the survivors reach their destination, they are surprised to learn that their captive is now an important figure in trying to get the French out of Algeria. The captain is enraged and wants to kill the man, but thinks better of it.

Commando (Tempo Film/Ficit/Galatea/Midega/Monarchia-Zeyn Film, 1962)
Lobby card

L'INSOUMIS
(THE DRAFT DODGER)

Citra/Cité Films/Delbeau (France). Released 1964. 115mins. Director: Alain Cavalier. Photography: Claude Renoir. Music: Georges Delerue. Screenplay: Jean Cau. Editor: Pierre Gillette. Production Design: Bernard Evein. Sound: Antoine Bonfanti. Cast: Alain Delon, Lea Massari, Maurice Garrell, Guy Laroche, Georges Géret, Robert Castel.

Synopsis: A man joins the Foreign Legion, then deserts and becomes involved with another deserter to rescue a leftist woman lawyer who has been kidnapped by terrorists in Algeria.

I PREDONI DEL SAHARA
(PLUNDERERS OF THE SAHARA)

King Film Prod./Copro Film (Italy). Released 1965. 92mins. Director: Guido Malatesta (James Reed). Screenplay: Ambrogio Molteni, from the novel by Emilio Salgari. Photography: Mario Montuori (Brad Novak). Producer: Roberto Lodovici. Production Design: Demofilo Fidani. Costumes: Mila Vitelli. Music: Angelo Francesco Lavagnino. Editor: Frank Robertson. Cast: George Mikell, Pamela Tudor, William Stockridge (Enzo

Subtitled Sands: Foreign Foreign Legion Films

Fiermonte), Furio Meniconi, John Drake (Nino Fuscagni), Farida Fahmy, Salah Nazni, Carl Tamblyn (Carlo Tamberlani), Nello Pazzafini.

Synopsis: A famous archaeologist is kidnapped by Arabs who hold him and his children hostage so that they can get information about a fabulous treasure. An adventurer who had served as a guide for the scientist frees them and takes them to a Legion fort. The Arabs overrun the undermanned fort, but the adventurer manages to keep his charges safe until reinforcements arrive. He then kills the Arab chieftain in a duel and wins the hand of one of the archaeologist's daughters.

LE FACTEUR S'EN VA-T-EN GUERRE
(THE MAILMAN GOES TO WAR)

J.J. Vital/Alcinter/Regina S.A. (France). Released August 10, 1966. 95mins. Color. Director: Claude Bernard-Aubert. Screenplay: René Hardy, based on the novel by Gaston Jean Gauthier. Photography: Marcel Grignon. Music: Georges Garvarentz. Editor: Gabriel Rongier. Cast: Charles Aznavour, Daniel Ceccaldi, Helmut Schneider, Doudou Babet, Jess Hahn, Jacques Richard, Lucien Barjon, Nop Nem, Michel Galabru, Maria Minh, Franco Fabrizi.

Synopsis: A Parisian postman decides to deliver mail in the army. He ends up with the Foreign Legion fighting in Indochina. He is captured by the Communists and eventually freed. He returns home with the Cambodian woman with whom he has fallen in love.

FOLLOW THAT CAMEL

Rank Film Distribution (Great Britain). Released December 14, 1967. 95mins. Director: Gerald Thomas. Producer: Peter Rogers. Writer: Talbot Rothwell. Photography: Alan Hume. Music: Eric Rogers. Editor: Alfred Roome. Art Director: Alex Vetchinsky. Cast: Phil Silvers, Jim Dale, Charles Hawtrey, Kenneth Williams, Anita Harris, Joan Sims, Bernard Bresslaw, Angela Douglas, Peter Butterworth, John Bluthal, William Mervyn, Peter Gilmore, Vincent Ball, Dany Robin, Marianne Stone, Michael Ward, Leon Greene, David Davenport, Richard Shaw, Valerie Van Ost, Jennifer Clulow, Jacqueline Pearce, Julian Orchard, Joan Ingram, Elspeith March, Billy Cornelius, Nikki van der Zyl, Ronnie Brody, Diana MacNamara, Monica Dietrich, Anna Willoughby, Penny Keen, Christine Pryor, June Cooper.

Variety, January 1, 1967: "It all works with considerable bounce, with elements of parody of Beau Geste-style movies for those alert to them."

Synopsis: An entry in the popular and long-running "Carry On" series. A young hero who is accused of cheating at cricket enlists, along with his manservant, in the Foreign Legion in order to atone for his disgrace. There, he encounters a sergeant who manufactures acts of heroism and has the decorations for them, a German commanding officer and a busty temptress. The Legion engages in running skirmishes with an Arab chieftain whose master is one Mustapha Leak. After a forced march through the arid desert, a comedic battle occurs at a desert fort.

A PROPOS DE CAMERONE
(ABOUT CAMERONE)
(France). Released 1969. 14mins.

Synopsis: Documentary about the Legion and the battle of Camerone.

A HALHATATLAN LEGIOSAKIT
(THE IMMORTAL LEGIONARY)
MAFILM (Hungary). Released September 9, 1971. 97mins. Color with tinted scenes. Director: Tamas Somlo. Writer: Jeno Rejto. Screenplay: Tamas Somlo. Cinematography: Tibor Banok. Editor: Luca Karall. Art Director: Jozsef Romvari. Costume Designer: Fanny Kemenes. Sound: Mihaly Lehmann. Consultant: Gyula Maar. Production Managers: Andras Nemeth, Istvan Daubner. Cast: Part I *Biography*: Lajos Ioze, Virag Dory, Karoly Kovacs, Istvan Szatmari, Marta Bako, Arpad Tery, Gyula Kery, Jozsef Vandor, Karoly Gyulay, Bela Both, Tivadar Horvath, Kornel Gelley, Alfonzo, Ferenc G. Deak, Andor Kolozsvari, Iza Sandor, Gabor Harsanyi, Sandor Suka, Istvan Szilagyi, Zoltan Gera, Janos Gosztonyi, Erno Szenasi, Erno Szabo, Janos Pasztor, Istvan Uri, Gyorgy Sandor, Vilmos Izsof, Endre Csonka, Mihaly Viola. Cast: Part II, *The Invisible Legion*: Alfonzo, Gyula Kery, Ilus Vay, Gyorgy Reinitz, Gellért Raksanyi.

Synopsis: This film combines details from writer Jenos Rejto's real life and two of his novels.

IL SERGENTE KLEMS
(SERGEANT KLEMS)
(MAN OF LEGEND)
Julia Film/Panta (Italy). Released 1971. 96mins. Director: Sergio Grieco. Screenplay: Bruno Di Geronimo, S. Grieco, Francesco Mazzei, based upon the biography by Paolo Zappa. Photography: Stelvio Massi. Music: Carlo Rustichelli. Editor: Gabrio Astori. Costume Design: Mario Giorsi. Producer: F. Mazzei. Cast: Peter Strauss, Tina Aumont, Pier Paolo Capponi, Massimo Serato, Rossella Como, Dada Gallotti, Franco Ressel, Pasquale Basile, Peter Berling, Luciana Paluzzi, Howard Ross, Massimo Righi, Mario Donen, Hassiba Rochdi, Hattar Eddhir, Jazia Klibi, Hamrouni Abdellatif.

Synopsis: A German soldier escapes being executed as a spy during World War I. Joining the Foreign Legion, he is sent to Morocco, but he deserts and joins the Riffs. He becomes a hero of the rebellion, marrying a chieftain's daughter. Later captured by the French, he is sent to Devil's Island, where he dies.

This film is a real hybrid, as it has scenes with the Spanish Foreign Legion and the Spahis.

MARCH OR DIE
Associated General Films /ITC/Columbia (Great Britain). Released August 5, 1977 (U.S.). 106mins. Color. Director: Dick Richards. Screenplay: David Z. Goodman. Story: David Z. Goodman, Dick Richards. Photography: John Alcott. Editor: O. Nicholas Brown. Music: Maurice Jarré. Art Direction: José Maria Tapiador. Set Decoration: Julian Mateos, Dennis J. Parrish. Costumes: Gitt Magrini. Makeup: José Antonio Sanchez. Hair Stylist: Blanca

Sanchez. Special Effects: Robert MacDonald. Production Design: Gil Parrondo. Producers: Dick Richards, Jerry Bruckheimer. Music Performed By the National Philharmonic Orchestra and Military Band of Garde Republicaine. Cast: Gene Hackman, Catherine Deneuve, Max Von Sydow, Terence Hill, Ian Holm, Jack O'Halloran, Rufus, Marcel Bozzuffi, Andre Penvern, Paul Sherman, Vernon Dobtcheff, Wolf Kohler, Walter Gotell, Albert Woods, Guy Deghy, Arnold Diamond, Marne Maitland, Gigi Bonds, Mathias Hell, Jean Champion, Paul Antrim, Catherine Willmer, Maurice Anden, Liliane Rovere, Elisabeth Mortensen, Leila Shenna, Jean Rougerie, Guy Mairesse, Eve Brenner, Guy Moily, Francoise Valorbe, Villena, Ernest Misko, Margaret Modlin.

March or Die (Assoc. General Films/ITC/Columbia, 1977) Lobby card

Time, August 22, 1977: "Director Dick Richards...moves the gory battle scenes along positively briskly....its limitation as well as its achievement is that it faithfully re-creates the sand-blown Legion epics of the 1930s."

New York Daily News, August 6, 1977: "It's as if Richards had deliberately stripped the movie of romantic appeal...the characters are only dimly defined."

Synopsis: A decimated Legion regiment returns to France at the end of World War I. Its battle-hardened major, an American, is then assigned to a post in Morocco where he learns that an archaeological dig begun before the war in Efroud has become the site of a massacre of a Legion company by Moroccan tribesmen under El Krim, with whom he is acquainted. He is ordered to guard the dig with his company. En route there, his train is halted by El Krim, who shows him the two curators of the dig. They have been blinded and had their tongues cut out and are kept in cages. The major mercifully shoots both of them. The major has his differences with the new curator. When the latter makes a major discovery of the casket of a figure holy to the locals, the major has it returned to El Krim as a peace offering. El Krim does not accept it as such, and later attacks Efroud in a bloody battle during which the major is killed. El Krim allows the Legion survivors to return to their post so that the world may know what has occurred there and why.

ET VIVE LA LIBERTE!
(AND LONG LIVE LIBERTY!)

Belstar Productions (France). Released February 1, 1978. 90mins. Color. Director: Serge Korber. Producer: Jacques Dorfmann. Cinematography: Jean-Jacques Tarbé. Screenplay: Jacques Lanzmann. Story: Albert Kantof, S. Korber. Editor: Marie-Claire Korber. Music: Paul DeSenneville, Olivier Toussaint. Cast: Gerard Rinaldi, Gerard Filipelli, Jean Sarrus, Philippe Brizard, Dani, Claude Piéplu, Georges Geret, Pierre Maguelon, Evelyne Ker, Bernard Dumaine, Jean-Louis Tristan, Henri Attal, Antione Valli, Leon Zitrone, Fernand Legros, Paul Mercey, Alain David, Marc de Jonge, Luc Florian.

Synopsis: Five members of the comedy team "Les Charlots" are in the French Foreign Legion. They are kidnapped while on a mission and emerge as heroes. As civilians, they become gamekeepers in a remote French estate where they are attacked by legionnaires led by their old commander.

LA LEGION SAUTE SUR KOLWEZI
(THE LEGION JUMPS ON KOLWEZI)

Bela/SNC/FR3--GEF-CCFC (France). Released January 9, 1980. 100mins. Color. Director: Raoul Cotard. Screenplay, Adaptation and Dialogue: André G. Brunelin, based on the novel by Pierre Sergent   Photography: Georges Liron, Jean Garcenot. Music: Serge Frankin. Editor: Michel Lewin. Supervision: Michel Laurent. Asst. Directors: Fred Runel, Philippe Charigot. Cast: Bruno Cremer, Laurent Malet, Mimsy Farmer, Giuliano Gemma, Jacques Perrin, Pierre Vaneck, Robert Etcheverry, Jean-Claude Bouillon, Pierre Rousseau, Gerard Essomba, Laure Moutoussamy, Patricia Lavidang, Henri Marteau, Jean Le Mouel.

Synopsis: The Foreign Legion comes to the aid of 3,000 European and American civilian hostages in the town of Kolwezi in Zaire. They are being held by local rebel forces and subjected to various ordeals.

FAUT S'LES FAIRE...CES LEGIONNAIRES!
(LEGIONNAIRES ARE REALLY SOMETHING!)

Stardust Productions/Carthago Films/Planfilm per Variety 7 (France). Released April 8, 1981. 86mins. Color. Director: Alain Nauroy. Screenplay and Dialogue: Victor Boniard.

Photography: Claude Bécognwée. Music: Jean-Pierre Doering. Editor: Gerard Le Du. Supervision: Yves Osmu. Producer: Catherine Bouguereau. Cast: Henri Garcin, Dany Carrel, André Valardy, Jean-Claude Martin, Jacques Bouanich, Eddy Jabes, Daniel Derval, Jean-Pierre Beccacci, Michel Feniou.

LES MORFALOUS
(THE GLUTTONOUS ONES)

Cérito Films-Soprofilms-V Films-Carthago Films/A.A.A. Cérito René Chateau (France). Released March 28, 1984. 95mins. Color. Director: Henri Verneuil. Screenplay Adaptation: H. Verneuil, Pierre Siniac, from the novel by Siniac. Photography: Edmond Séchan. Dialogue: Michel Audiard. Costumes: Paulette Breil. Editor: Pierre Gillette. Music: Georges Delerue. Production Design: Jacques Maumont, Alain Sempé. Cast: Jean-Paul Belmondo, Jacques Villeret, Michel Constantin, Michel Creton, Mathias Habbich, Marie Laforet, Francois Perrot, Maurice Auzel, Gerard Buhr, John David, Jr., Robert Lombard, Peter Selmer, Caroline Sihol.

Synopsis: In 1943 a Foreign Legion battalion is given the task of removing a fortune in gold bullion from the vault of a bank in a North African town before it falls into German hands. As they arrive at the town, they are ambushed by the Germans and only three legionnaires survive. They still manage to defeat the Germans.

IL ETAIT UNE FOIS UNE LEGION
(ONCE UPON A TIME THERE WAS A LEGION)

(France). Released 1989. 60mins. Director: Marton Ledniczky. Photography: Sandor Kardos. Screenplay: Csaba Kardos and Marton Ledniczky. Editor: Teri Losonczi. Music: Ferenc Darvas. Cast: Gyorgy Cserhalmi, Samuel Lebihan, Istvan Bubik, Isa Mercure, Amelie Pick and former Legionnaires.

Fictional documentary about the life of a typical legionnaire.

MY LEGION
(MA LEGION, MEINE LEGION)

Budapest Filmstudio-MTV/FMS/MAFILM/BBS/KERSZI (Hungary). Released 1989. 86mins. Color. Director: Marton Ledniczky. Writers: Csaba Kardos and M. Ledniczky. Photography: Andras Mesz, Lorand Mertz, Tibor Klopfler. Editor: Teri Losohczi. Production Managers: Andras Ozorai, Daniel Vaissaire, Rezso Bodonyi, Andras Toth.

A documentary about the Legion.

DIEN BIEN PHU

Mods Films-Flach Film-Antenne 2/Films A2 (France). Released March 4, 1992. Color. 140mins. Director: Pierre Schoendoerffer. Screenplay: Pierre Schoendoerffer. Producer: Jacques Kirsner. Photography: Bernard Lutic. Music: Georges Delerue. Editor: Armand Psenny. Asst. Directors: Frédérick Schoendorffer, Jean-Charles Smith, Madame Bach Diep.

Special Effects: Oliver Zeneski, Jean-Pierre Maricourt. Costumes: Olga Pelettier. Cast: Donald Pleasance, Ludmilla Mikael, Patrick Catalifo, Jean-Francois Balmer, Raoul Billerey, Christopher Buchholz, Francois Negret, Maxime Leroux, Igor Hossein, Luc Lavandier, Patrick Chauvel, Ludovic Schoendoerffer, Maité Nahyr.

Synopsis: An American reporter is caught between the French and Vietminh forces during the 57-day battle in French Indochina.

WARHEADS

Max Film/Eurocréation/WDR (France-Germany). Released January 26, 1992. 182mins. Color. Director: Romuald Karmakar. Writer: R. Karmakar. Photography: Michael Teutsch (Mississippi), Klaus Merkle (French Guiana), Reiner Lauter (Munich), Bruno Affret (Croatia). Editor: Katja Dringenberg. Producers: Wolfgang Pfeiffer, Anne-Marie Autissier. Sound: Klaus-Peter Kaiser (Mississippi), Norbert Werner (French Guiana), Eckert Kuchenbecker (Munich), Istvan Kerenyi (Croatia).

Documentary about mercenaries that includes the life of Gunter Aschenbrenner, a German legionnaire.

LE COMICHE 2
(THE COMICS 2)

CGG/Tiger (Italy). Released 1992. 91mins. Director: Neri Parenti. Story: Alessandro Bencivenni. Screenplay: A. Bencivenni. Cinematography: Allesandro D'Eva. Costumes: Fiamma Bedendo. Special Effects: Antonio Corridori, Franco Ragusa. Producers: Mario Cecchi Gori, Vittorio Cecchi Gori. Editor: Sergio Montanari. Music: Bruno Zambrini. Art Direction: Christine Onori, Maria Stilde Ambruzzi. Cast: Paolo Villagio, Renato Pozzetto, Roberto Della Casa, Paul Muller, Loredana Romito, Angelo Pellegrino, Alfiero Toppetti, Antonio Allocca, Giulia Donnini, Catherine Zago, Piero DiCarlo, John Armstead, Mario Barbaro, Romaro Puppo, Mohamed Salem Abdel.

ZHAN LONG ZAI YE
(U.S.: INVINCIBLE)

Win's Movie Prod. & I/E Co./Samico Films Prod. Co. Ltd. (Hong Kong). Released December 5, 1992. 96mins. Director: Blackie Ko Sau-Leung. Screenplay: Man Keung Chan, Yin Nam. Producer: Yeuk Yuen. Cinematography: Joe Chan, Po-Man Wong, Simon Li. Art Director: Jason Mok. Editor: Ki-Ho Chan. Cast: Wong Kit, Sharla Chung Man, Sau Leung "Blacky" Ko, Billy Blanks, Man Cheung, Danny Lee, Fong Lung, Stefanos Miltsakakis, Jerry Trimble, Sau Yat, Mak Wai Cheung.

Synopsis: During the Gulf War, a mild-mannered man kills a gangster who had been harassing his girlfriend. He flees to France where he enlists in the French Foreign Legion. After basic training, he is sent to Kuwait to help guard the royal family. He survives this mission and returns to Hong Kong in fighting trim, ready for revenge against the gang. His foes, however, have recruited some former legionnaires to deal with him.

The literal translation of the title is "Fighting Dragon in Field."

Subtitled Sands: Foreign Foreign Legion Films

ELITE FIGHTING FORCES: THE FRENCH FOREIGN LEGION
D. D. Video (Great Britain). Released 1993. 54mins. Color and Black and White. Director: Michael Du Monceau.

Documentary, part of a series.

A HAROM TESTOR AFRIKABAN
(THREE GUARDSMEN IN AFRICA)
Mahir Film Kft./Budafilm Kft./Magyar Televizio tamagoto supported by: Magyar MozgokepAlapitvany Postabank Rt., Magyar Kelkereskedelmi Bank Rt., Pasha Tours Szines (Hungary). Released October 3, 1996. 84mins. Color. Director: Istvan Bujtor. Screenplay: Istvan Bujtor. Cinematography: Janos Kende. Editor: Ferencne Szecsenyi. Art Director: Katalin Juhasz. Costume Designer: Hajnal Tordai. Music: Karoly Frenteisz. Sound: Istvan Sipos. Production Manager: Zoltan Meszaros. Producer: Istvan Bujtor. Cast: Gabor Koncz, Zoltan Ratoti, Bela Stenczer, Ferenc Kallai, Miklos Benedek, Istvan Szilagyi, Zsuzsa Nyertes, Ferenc Bacs, Gabor Reviczky.

Synopsis: Three legionnaires attempt to find the younger brother of a beautiful blonde. Upon learning that he is imprisoned in the penal colony in the middle of the desert, they manage to have themselves sent there. They are accompanied by an officer. At the colony, they discover idyllic conditions, but soon realize that a grandiose financial scheme lies behind the situation. They find the blonde's brother, as well as her father. They also discover that the blonde has been with them all along in disguise. They escape in order to forward the secret document which will unveil the scheme to the army brass. Through some chicanery, they manage to elude the colonial army and get the letter to its destination.

LEGION
Kushner-Locke/Conquistador Ent./Mahogany Pictures. Released 1998.

BEAU TRAVAIL
La Septe-Art/SM Films/Tanais Prods. (France). Released May 3, 2000. 90mins. Director: Claire Denis. Writers: Claire Denis and Jean Pol Fargeau, based on *Billy Budd* by Herman Melville. Director of Photography: Agnes Godard. Editor: Nelly Quettier. Music: Eran Tzur. Production Designer: Arnaud de Moleron. Producer: Jerome Minet. Cast: Gregoire Colin, Denis Lavant, Michel Subor, Marta Tafesse Kassa, Richard Courcet, Nicolas Devauchelle, Adiatou Massudi, Mickael Ravovski, Dan Herzbeth, Giuseppe Molino, Gianfranco Poddighe, Marc Veh, Thong Duy Nguyen, Jean-Yves Vivet, Bernando Montet, Dmitri Tsiapkinis, Djamel Zemali, Abdlekader. Shown at The New York Film Festival, September 28 and 29, 1999.

New York Times, September 28, 1999: "...a woman's rapt meditation on an all-male society....a film that has the sweep and esthetic power of a full-length ballet."

The Brooklyn Papers, April 14. 2003: "...Denis shows little interest in the sociology of this unique community, opting instead for frustrating abstraction. In strikingly shot but interminable sequences ...soldiers train beneath the sizzling sun..."

Synopsis: An officer is threatened by the arrival of a handsome and talented new recruit and sets out to sabotage his career.

SIMON, AN ENGLISH LEGIONNAIRE
(U.S.: *DESERTER*)

Simon Films (Great Britain). Released May 30, 2002. 90mins. Director: Martin Huberty. Writers: William M. Akers, Axel Aylwen. Photography: Dino Parks. Production Designer: Amanda Bernstein. Art Direction: Grant Armstrong. Cast: Paul Fox, Tom Hardy, Aitor Merino, Felicite de Jeu, Yorick van Wageringen, Bruno Munoz-Rojas, Javier Alenor, Christian Mulot, Dugald Bruce-Lockhart, Enzo Cilenti, Katie Jones, Kate Maberly.

Synopsis: An Englishman joins the Foreign Legion during Algeria's war for independence and learns the true meaning of heroism.

Deserter **(Simon Films, 2002)**

SATIRIC SANDS: COMEDIES AND CARTOONS

LES AMANTS DE MOGADOR
(*THE LOVERS OF MOGADOR*)
Dawliz/Poetiche Cinematografiche (Morocco/Italy). Released October 2003. 119mins. CinemaScope. Director: Souheil Ben Barka. Producer: Mouly A. Badri. Screenplay: Bernard Stora, S. Ben Barka. Photography: Vittorio Bagnasco. Art Directors: Enzo Medusa, Amal al Mazouni. Editor: Fatima Darsi. Music: Richard Horowitz, Sussan Deyhin. Special Effects: Gino de Rossi, Hassan Benabar. Cast: Max von Sydow, Mahmoud Mahmoudi, Violante Placido, Marie-Christine Barrault, Claude Rich, Bernard Fresson, Emmanuelle Vezzoli, Boujem Oujoud, Mohamed el Ouaradi, Fatima Attif, Abdellah Ferkoussi, Robert Clement-Jones, Alain Mirbeck, Antoine Mirbeck.

Variety, October 7, 2003: "...offers a vision of colonialism that is as old-fashioned as pic's swelling music, bad French dubbing, sadistic thin-lipped villain, and Omar Sharif look-a-like hero. Pic hits every cliché in the book..."

Synopsis: In Morocco in 1936-37 a company of legionnaires is slaughtered by Moroccan rebels. The rebel leader is captured by the French and brought to a hospital where he is visited by his brother, a rich merchant sympathetic to the rebel cause. There the merchant meets and falls in love with a young and feisty French Catholic nurse. She is shunned by her family and other Europeans and he by his countrymen. They manage to overcome all obstacles and marry, living happily together. Meanwhile, the Moroccan leader is wounded in a fight with the regular French army and seeks aid in the Legion. They use him as an interpreter. During a fierce battle where he refuses to shoot his fellow Moroccans, he saves the life of a legionnaire he has befriended and manages to escape the Legion and find his wife again in a distant region of Morocco.

§

CHAPTER EIGHT
Satiric Sands: Comedies and Cartoons

Like all good military institutions, the French Foreign Legion has come in for its share of spoofing. However, it seems to have suffered less at the hands of comics than other outfits. Only four noted comedy teams--Laurel and Hardy, the Three Stooges, Smith and Dale and Abbott and Costello--dared to tackle the famed fighting force. The first-named actually did so twice within a decade after Stan Laurel had starred in a one-reel spoof of Universal's 1922 version of *Under Two Flags* in 1923.

Filmography

UNDER TWO JAGS

Hal Roach-Pathé. Released June 3, 1923. 1 reel. Director: George Jeske. Producer: Hal Roach. Photography: Frank Young. Asst. Director: C. Brandenburg. Props: J. V. White. Cast: Stan Laurel, Katherine Grant, Mae Laurel, Sam Brooks, Charles Stevenson, William Gillespie, Roy Brooks, Eddie Baker.

Motion Picture News, June 2, 1923: "...a very enjoyable travesty of Ouida's well-known novel *Under Two Flags.* The original story is followed broadly...The mock characterizations...are very amusing...."

Synopsis: A stranger appears at a Legion outpost and enlists in the Legion. Cheroot, "the daughter of the regiment," falls in love with him. The man meets Princess, who also falls for him, and utilizes his talent for whittling to create a set of dinner knives for her. When the commanding officer is cut by one of the knives, he orders the recruit to be shot at sunrise and a grave is prepared. Cheroot saves the man, however, and the officer falls into the grave instead.

SHE'S A SHEIK
Paramount. Released November 12, 1927. 6 reels. Director: Clarence Badger. Story: John MacDermott. Photography: J. Roy Hunt. Scenario: Lloyd Corrigan and Grover Jones, from a story by John McDermott. Intertitles: George Marion, Jr. Cast: Bebe Daniels, Richard Arlen, William Powell, Josephine Dunn, James Bradbury, Jr., Bill Franey, Paul McAllister, Al Fremont.

Moving Picture World, November 26, 1927: "...is a combination lampoon on 'The Sheik' and 'Beau Geste' with a little Douglas Fairbanks on the side....it is clever foolery, with a well-spaced succession of laughs..."

Synopsis: The daughter of a Spanish mother and an Arabian sheik will have only a Christian for a husband. When her selection seems indifferent to the honor, she kidnaps him. She eventually wins him when she saves a French detachment in a border war.

PLASTERED IN PARIS
Fox. Released September 23, 1928. 6 reels. Director: Benjamin Stoloff. Producer: William Fox. Story: Harry Sweet and Lou Breslow. Screenplay: Harry Brand and Andy Rice. Photography: Charles Clarke. Dialogue: Edwin Burke. Titles: Malcolm S. Boylan. Cast: Samuel Cohen, Jack Pennick, Lola Salvi, Ivan Linow, Hugh Allan, Marion Byron, Michael Visaroff, Albert Conti, August Tollaire.

New York Times, September 24, 1928: "It is in most of its episodes a nightmare, an animated caricature with fine photography and competent acting...The strategic attack of the Foreign Legion on the Riffians [sic] and the rescue of a young woman...are depicted in a highly amusing fashion."

Synopsis: Two American veterans of the Great War return to the U.S. for an American Legion convention ten years later. One of them believes a war wound has turned him into a kleptomaniac and his friend makes him see a specialist, who does him no good. The two are later mistakenly drafted into the French Foreign Legion and end up rescuing a commandant's daughter from a harem.

LOVE TAILS OF MOROCCO
M-G-M. Released September 5, 1931. 20mins. A Dogville Comedy. Directors: Jules White, Zion Myers.

Featuring an all-canine cast. They give their reasons for having joined the Legion, told in flashbacks.

BEAU HUNKS
M-G-M. Released December 12, 1931. 4 reels. Director: James W. Horne. Producer: Hal Roach. Photography: Art Lloyd and Jack Stevens. Editor: Richard Currier. Dialogue: H. M. Walker. Sound: Elmer R. Raguse. Cast: Stan Laurel, Oliver Hardy, Charles Middleton, Charlie Hall, Stanley Sandford, Harry Schultz, Gordon Douglas, Sam Lufkin, Marvin Hatley,

Jack Hill, Leo Willis, Bob Kortman, Baldwin Cooke, Dick Gilbert, Oscar Morgan, Ham Kinsey, Broderick O' Farrell, James Horne.

Synopsis: Ollie receives a note from his girlfriend telling him their affair is over. Distraught, he and Stan join the Foreign Legion to forget her. In the barracks there, they notice that several other enlistees all have the same photo, including the commandant, who has a large blow-up of it on his wall! After a brief training period, their outfit is sent to relieve Fort Arid, which is about to be attacked by a large force of Riffs. When the Riffs break through the gate, Stan and Ollie find a large cache of kegs filled with nails, which they strew over the ground, disabling the barefooted Riffs. They capture the Riff leader; while disarming him, they discover the photo of Ollie's former girlfriend in his robe. (The photo is of starlet Jean Harlow [1911-1937], who was a Roach contract player before being signed by M-G-M and gaining fame as "The Platinum Blonde" in the 1930s.)

One line in this spoof was objected to by the French government: "The Legion is hell on earth and in heaven." They insisted on its removal and the producers complied.

Beau Hunks (M-G-M, 1931) Oliver Hardy, unknown actor, Stan Laurel

ARABIAN SHRIEKS

Paramount. Released March 4, 1932. 22mins. Director: Aubrey Scotto. Story: A. Scotto and Harry W. Conn. Cast: Joe Smith, Charlie Dale.

Motion Picture Herald, February 13, 1932: "Smith and Dale save the day for the Foreign Legion in their own peculiar, and rather amusing, manner."

Synopsis: In the French Foreign Legion, Smith and Dale accidentally volunteer for spy duty. They penetrate a sheik's hideout and save the fort.

Filmed at Paramount's Astoria Studio in New York, this short used stock footage from the 1926 version of *Beau Geste*.

HATTA MARRI

Mack Sennett/Educational Film Exchange, Inc. Released July 10, 1932. 20mins. Director: Babe Stafford. Photography: John W. Boyle, George Unholz. Cast: Harry Gribbon, Marjorie Kane, Dorothy Granger, Marvin Lobach, Dave Silverstein, Ethella Blanche, Johnny Rand.

ARABIAN TIGHTS

Hal Roach. Released June 3, 1933. 20mins. Director: Hal Roach. Editor: William H. Terhune. Photography: Len Powers. Music: Leroy Shield. Songs: "Mademoiselle from Armentieres," "I'll Forget You." Cast: Charley Chase, Eddie Baker, Russ Powell, Muriel Evans, Carlton Griffin, Harry Schultz, Jerry Bergen, Rolfe Sedan, Jimmy Adams, The Ranch Boys.

Synopsis: Chase and his pals accidentally join the Legion while running out on paying a beer tab. While marching through the desert, they are lured to an oasis by what they think are dancing girls. The "girls" turn out to be some sheik's men; Chase and his friends are caught and imprisoned. Impressed by their singing, the sheik makes plans to get them out of the Legion so that he and they can set up a business in the United States, something the sheik has wanted to do.

WE'RE IN THE LEGION NOW

Grand National. Released January 16, 1937. 56mins. Hirlicolor. Director: Crane Wilbur. Producer: George A. Hirliman. Screenplay: Roger Whateley, from *The Rest Cure* by J. D. Newsom. Photography: Mack Stengler, A.S.C. Editor: Tony Martinelli. Makeup: Max Factor. Art Directors: Lewis Rachmil and Frank Sylos. Asst. Director: John Price. Assoc. Producers: Charles Hunt, Louis Rantz. Additional Dialogue: Crane Wilbur. Musical Direction: A. F. Meyer. Production Manager: Sam Diego. Dance Director: Arthur Dreifus. Dance Costumes: Helen Rose. Wardrobe: Western Costume Co. Cast: Reginald Denny, Esther Ralston, Vince Barnett, Eleanor Hunt, Claudia Dell, Robert Frazer, Rudolph Armendt, Francisco Moran, Merril McCormack, Frank Hoyt, Manuel Pelufo, Charles Moyer, Lou Hicks. Originally released by Regal in 1936 as *Rest Cure*.

Satiric Sands: Comedies and Cartoons

We're in the Legion Now (Grand National, 1937) Rudolph Anders, Vince Barnett, Eleanor Hunt, Reginald Denny

Variety, June 9, 1937: "...looks like an effort to apply the Hirliman method of western opus to a combo gangster-Foreign Legion affair. Quickie aspects of the production are discernible in the desert and native village shots, obviously from newsreels."

Synopsis: Two New York gangsters flee to Paris to avoid rivals after Prohibition is repealed. There they run afoul of a Legion officer when they accidentally meet his wife and sister-in-law. They spot one of their rivals and are advised by the latter to join the Legion. They enlist and are sent to Morocco, as is the Legion officer. There they make enemies of their sergeant who happens to like the same American café singer they do. Sent to a penal camp, they become involved in a mutiny just before a visit by the officer and the ladies, who are being chased by a band of Arabs. In the ensuing battle, they acquit themselves well, earning a revocation of their sentences as well as promotions.

A Spanish-language version was also produced by Hirliman and released in 1935. Directed by John Reinhardt, it was called *De La Sarten Al Fuego* (*From the Frying Pan into the Fire*), ran 82 minutes and starred Juan Toreno, Romuldo Tirado and Rosita Moreno.

We're in the Legion Now (Grand National, 1937) **Title card**

WEE WEE MONSIEUR
Columbia. Released February 18, 1938. 17mins. Director: Del Lord. Producer: Jules White. Photography: Andre Barlatier. Editor: Charles Nelson. Screenwriter: Searle Kramer. Cast: The Three Stooges, Bud Jamison, Vernon Dent, William Irving, John Lester Johnson, Harry Semels, Ethelreda Leopold. Working title: *The Foreign Legioneers*

Motion Picture Exhibitor, February 15, 1938: "Typical of the Stooges who continue their mad antics to their followers' complete satisfaction."

Synopsis: The Stooges are artists in Paris behind in their rent who hope to sell a painting to make their rent. When their landlord threatens to kill them, they flee and try to join the American Legion, but wind up enlisting in the French Foreign Legion instead. When their captain is kidnapped, they dress up as Santa Clauses, then as harem girls, and rescue him.

THE FLYING DEUCES
RKO Radio Pictures. Released October 20, 1939. 69mins. Director: A. Edward Sutherland. Producer: Boris Morros. Production Manager: Joe Nadel. Second Unit Director: Robert Stillman. Photography: Art Lloyd. Original Story and Screenplay: Ralph Spence, Alfred Schiller, Charles Rogers and Harry Langdon. Art Direction: Boris Leven. Editor: Jack

Dennis. Musical Direction: Edward Paul. Musical Compositions: John Leipold and Leo Shuken. Aerial Photography: Elmer Dyer. Photographic Effects: Howard Anderson. Chief Pilot and Technical Advisor: Frank Clarke. Cast: Stan Laurel, Oliver Hardy, Jean Parker, Reginald Gardiner, James Finlayson, Charles Middleton, Jean del Val, Clem Wilenchick, Richard Cramer, Michael Visaroff, Monica Bannister, Bonnie Bannon, Jane Carey, Christine Cabanne, Frank Clarke, Eddie Borden, Sam Lufkin, Kit Guard, Billy Engle, Jack Chefe.

Wee Wee Monsieur **(Columbia, 1938) Moe, Curly, Larry**

The Flying Deuces **(RKO, 1939) Stan and Ollie try to blend in.**

Motion Picture Exhibitor, October 18, 1939: "...typical Laurel and Hardy hokum injected into a thin story idea."

New York Times, November 24, 1939: "The story is a situation and little more...The boys are still indulging in their...same old comedy routines...."

The Flying Deuces (RKO, 1939) Poster

SATIRIC SANDS: COMEDIES AND CARTOONS

Synopsis: Ollie enlists in the Foreign Legion to forget a woman whom he discovers is already married and is joined by Stan. There he meets the woman again, when she comes to visit her husband, a Legion officer. Arrested for desertion, the pair escapes in a plane. The plane crashes and Ollie is killed, but is reincarnated as a horse.

ABBOTT AND COSTELLO IN THE FOREIGN LEGION

Universal-International. Released July 24, 1950. 80mins. Director: Charles Lamont. Writers: John Grant, Leonard Stern and Martin Ragaway, based on a story by D. D. Beauchamp. Photography: George Robinson. Music: Joseph Gershenson. Producer: Robert Arthur. Editor: Frank Gross. Art Directors: Bernard Herzbrun, Eric Orbom. Makeup: Bud Westmore. Special Photography: David S. Horsley. Hair Stylist: Joan St. Oegger. Set Decorators: Russell A. Gausman, Ray Jeffers. Cast: Bud Abbott, Lou Costello, Patricia Medina, Walter Slezak, Douglass Dumbrille, Leon Belasco, Marc Lawrence, Wee Willie Davis, Tor Johnson, Sam Menacker, Fred Numey, Paul Fierro, Henry Corden, Jack Raymond, Jack Shutta, Harry Wilson, Ernesto Morelli, Jack Davidson, Chuck Hamilton, Dan Seymour, Alberto Monn, John Cliff, Guy Beach, Peter Ortiz, Ted Hecht, Mahmud Shaikaly, Charmienne Harker, David Gorcey.

Abbott and Costello in the Foreign Legion (Universal-International, 1950) Title card

Harrison's Reports, July 15, 1950: "...the story is insipid and the comedy situations are... milked for much more than they are worth. ...the action has a tendency to lag."

Synopsis: Abbott and Costello are wrestling promoters. When one of their wrestlers, Abdullah, runs off to Algeria, they go after him to bring him back. There they become involved in a plot by Arabs trying to stop the French from building a railroad. A traitorous Foreign Legion sergeant tricks them into enlisting in the Legion for five years. After going through training, they become part of a relief patrol sent to a besieged fort. While they are outside their camp, the patrol is wiped out in a night attack. They are later caught by the tribal leader and condemned to death. They are to be torn apart by two wrestlers, one of whom turns out to be Abdullah. He's glad to see them, for he wants to go back to Brooklyn so he doesn't have to marry the sheik's ugly daughter. He plots with Lou to escape after creating much confusion among the Arabs. They get away in a jeep, but are pursued by the Arabs. Upon reaching the fort, they are fired upon by a relief column of legionnaires. After a chase about the fort, they trick the Arabs into entering the fort and then accidentally blow it up. The pair is given citations and honorable discharges.

TEN TALL MEN

Hecht-Norma/Columbia. Released January 26, 1951. 97mins. Color. Director: Willis Goldbeck. Screenplay: Roland Kibbee and Frank Davis, from an original story by James Warner Bellah and Willis Goldbeck. Producer: Harold Hecht. Photography: William Snyder, A.S.C. Art Director: Carl Anderson. Music: David Buttolph. Musical Director: Morris Stoloff. Editor: William Lyon, A.C.E. Set Decorator: Louis Diage. Asst. Director: Earl Bellamy. Makeup: Clay Campbell. Hair Stylist: Helen Hunt. Gowns: Jean Louis. Cast: Burt Lancaster, Gilbert Roland, Jody Lawrence, Kieron Moore, Mike Mazurki, George Tobias, John Dehner, Nick Dennis, Gerald Mohr, Ian MacDonald, Mari Blanchard, Donald Randolph, Raymond Greenleaf, Stephen Bekassy, Robert Clary, Henry Rowland, Michael Pate, Paul Marion, Henri Letondal, Philip Van Zandt, Joy Windsor, JoAnn Arnold, Edith Sheets, Diana Dawson, Gwen Caldwell, Helen Reichman, George Khoury, Nick Cravat, Shimen Ruskin, Carlo Tricoli, Tom Conroy, Alan Ray, Frank Arnold, Ralph Volkie, Mickey Simpson, Charlita, Rita Conde, Benny Burt.

Exhibitor, November 7, 1951: "It's entertaining, suspenseful, and interest-holding. The pace is fast, the acting credible, and the production and direction okeh."

Harrison's Reports, October 27, 1951: "It is colorful...the action is mostly fast, but it has little human interest or heart appeal. The mood is mostly light and flippant...."

Synopsis: Three adventurous legionnaires, a sergeant, a corporal and an enlisted man, volunteer for any dangerous assignment. After bringing in a Riff chieftain as captive, the sergeant is caught romancing the lieutenant's lady friend. The officer strikes her with his riding crop and is decked by the sergeant. The latter is thrown into jail, where he befriends the captured Riff chieftain. The Riff tells the sergeant of an impending Riff attack on the city, which is currently undermanned. The sergeant asks for a squad of prisoners to divert the attention of the Riffs for the five days it will take reinforcements to arrive. He is given his two friends and seven prisoners. If he succeeds, he and the others will earn their freedom.

Ten Tall Men (Hecht-Norma/Columbia, 1951) Insert

Disguised as tribesmen, they enter a Riff camp, where they learn that an alliance between two enemy tribes is to be formed by the marriage of a sheik's daughter and a tribal leader. The sergeant decides to kidnap the sheik's daughter for five days, figuring the Riffs will take time to find her and delay their attack. The sergeant treats the woman well, but she manages to seduce one of his men and escapes. He tries to kill the sergeant, but her cry warns him, and as the man flees, he is shot by a Riff scout, who is in turn shot by a legionnaire. Left alone, the woman starts a fire, alerting the Riffs to the legionnaires' location. The legionnaires lose another man during the ensuing fight in a sandstorm. After the fight, the sergeant and the girl are surrounded by the Riffs and the former is captured. When the leader whom she is to marry attempts to torture the sergeant, the girl says the marriage will not occur unless he lets the legionnaire go. The sergeant is freed and returns to his men. Later, disguised as Riffs, they attend the wedding ceremony and create a commotion which evolves into a donnybrook. In the confusion, the girl is taken by her husband-to-be and threatened with a hot poker when the sergeant confronts him. The girl makes a sudden move, freeing herself, and the sergeant and the leader grapple. The latter is burned in the face with the poker. The sergeant and the girl are married at the Legion post.

THE LAST REMAKE OF BEAU GESTE

Universal. Released July 15, 1977. 85mins. Technicolor and Panavision. Director: Marty Feldman. Producer: William S. Gilmore. Screenplay: Marty Feldman, Chris Allen. Story: Marty Feldman, Sam Bobrick. Photography: Gerry Fisher, B.S.C. Art Director: Les Dilley. Editors: Jim Clark, Arthur Schmidt. Music: John Morris. Production Design: Brian Eatwell. Set Decorator: Roger Christian. Costumes: May Routh. First Asst. Director: Tom Joyner. Special Visual Effects: Albert Whitlock. Special Effects Supervisor: John Stears. Stunt Coordinator: Buddy Van Horn. Choreographer: Irving Davies. Makeup: Del Armstrong. Second Asst. Director: Vincent Winter. Executive Producers: Howard West, George Shapiro. Wardrobe Master: Ron Beck. Cast: Marty Feldman, Ann-Margret, Michael York, Peter Ustinov, James Earl Jones, Trevor Howard, Henry Gibson, Terry-Thomas, Roy Kinnear, Spike Milligan, Avery Schreiber, Hugh Griffith, Irene Handl, Sinead Cusack, Henry Polic II, Ted Cassidy, Burt Kwouk, Val Pringle, Gwen Nelson, Philip Bollard, Nicholas Bridge, Michael McConkey, Bekhi Bridge, Roland MacLeod, Martin Snaric, Stephen Lewis, Ed McMahon. Filmed in Ireland and Spain.

Time, August 8, 1977: "Feldman has a keen eye for the sillier conventions of movie narrative.... there are enough imaginative gags and such a pleasantly adolescent spirit about the film as to warrant looking in on it...."

Newsweek, July 25, 1977: "...is largely a movie about other movies....harmless vulgarity, friendly, low-key performances from a genial cast, and well-meaning but unexceptional physical comedy...."

Synopsis: A very valuable sapphire is coveted by members of the Geste family, including the father's new young wife. When the father takes to his deathbed, Beau Geste steals the stone to keep his stepmother from getting it. He flees to North Africa, where he joins the French Foreign Legion. His brother Digby follows him and also enlists. The stepmother also follows him. At a Legion fort, the brothers experience a number of comic situations and have to deal with a commanding officer with a metal leg.

The Last Remake of Beau Geste (Universal, 1977) **Peter Ustinov's stunt double and Michael York**

Oddly, this is the only film based on Wren to portray Beau and Digby as twins, which they are in the book. This is part of the humor, though, given the disparate looks of actors York and Feldman. Feldman purchased the rights to the 1939 version, utilizing footage from it in his production.

JEWEL OF THE SAHARA
Keyser Productions. Released 2001. 17mins. Color. Director: Ariel Vromen. Writers: Alon Aranya and Kennedy Taylor. Cinematography: Gerardo M. Madrazo. Editor: Ariel Vromen. Music: Gahl Sasson. Production Design: Erica Vilardi. Costumes: Erica Vilardi. Cast: Gerard Butler, Clifford David, Peter Franzen, Ori Pfeffer, Nicholl Hiren, Ralph Lister, Gian Saragosa, Ari Auerbach, Gahl Sasson, Rodrigo Mandrazo, Tomer Almagor, Leonal Renard, Gili Pinchuck, Santiago Barriero, Kevin Keyser.

Synopsis: A squad of legionnaires led by a British officer becomes stranded in the Sahara Desert in the 1950s and their camel receives some unwanted attention after the homesick officer reads some steamy love letters from his wife.

The Last Re-make of Beau Geste (Universal, 1977) **Poster**

Satiric Sands: Comedies and Cartoons

Cartoons

Beau Best. Universal. Released May 22, 1933. 6mins. A Snappy Production. Direction and Animation: Walter Lantz and William Nolan. Cast: Oswald Rabbit. Synopsis: Oswald rescues a damsel in distress in the desert.

Beau Bosko. Warner Bros. Released July 1, 1933. 7mins. Producer/Director: Hugh Harman. Animation: Rollin Hamilton and Norman Blackburn. Cast: Bosko, Honey. Synopsis: Legionnaire Bosko is sent on a perilous mission to an Arab city. There he meets and saves Honey, a girl in perpetual distress.

Buddy of the Legion. Warner Bros. Released April 4, 1935. 7mins. Looney Tunes. Supervisor: Ben Hardaway. Animation: Bob Clampett and Charles Jones. Music: Bernard Brown. Cast: Buddy. Synopsis: Buddy falls asleep while reading a book about the Foreign Legion in the bookstore where he works. He dreams that he is a legionnaire captain whose troop has been lured into a fortress of Amazons. He attempts to save his men and others captured by the female warriors and wakes up in time to be fired.

Little Beau Porky. Warner Bros. Released October 24, 1936. Looney Tunes. Supervisor: Frank Tashlin. Animation: Robert Bentley and Nelson Demorest. Producer: Leon Schlesinger. Musical Direction: Carl W. Stalling. Cast: Porky Pig. Synopsis: Porky is a legionnaire private who is left behind by his commanding officer when his comrades go out on a mission. He ends up defending the fort alone against the evil sheik Ali Mode.

Ali Baba Bound. Warner Bros. Released February 10, 1940. Looney Tunes. Supervisor: Robert Clampett. Story: Melvin Miller. Animation: Vive Risto. Producer: Leon Schlesinger. Musical Direction: Carl W. Stalling. Cast: Porky Pig. Synopsis: Legionnaire Porky receives a secret message that Ali Baba and his Dirty Sleeves are about to attack the desert fort and sets out to warn the defenders. Arriving at the fort, he discovers that all the men have gone to a Legion convention in Boston. He is forced to defend the outpost with the aid of a baby camel and its mother.

Little Beau Pepé. Warner Bros. Released February 9, 1952. Merrie Melodies. Color. Director: Chuck Jones. Story: Michael Maltese. Animation: Lloyd Vaughan, Ben Washam, Ken Harris and Phil Monroe. Cast: Pepé Le Pew. Synopsis: Pepé Le Pew decides to join the Foreign Legion after his most recent unlucky love affair. At the Legion outpost the mascot accidentally has a white stripe painted down her back and Pepé mistakes her for a skunk. He chases her to the tent of a sheik near an oasis and wins her with the aid of some choice Arabian perfume and oil.

Sahara Hare. Warner Bros. Released March 26, 1955. Looney Tunes. Director: I. Freleng. Story: Warren Foster. Animation: Gerry Chinquy, Ted Bonnickson and Art Davis. Music: Milt Franklyn. Cast: Bugs Bunny, Yosemite Sam, cameo by Daffy Duck. Synopsis: Searching for Miami Beach, Bugs Bunny winds up tunneling to the Sahara Desert. There he encounters a desert bandit named Riff-Raff Sam and his oddball camel. Sam chases Bugs to a Legion fort and spends a lot of time trying to gain entry himself. He is finally blown up by a bomb which is connected to a series of doors.

Insultin' the Sultan. Color. 6mins. Air Date: September 1960. Syndicated. Director: Gene Deitch Producer: William L. Snyder. Voices: Jack Mercer, Mae Questel. Cast: Popeye, Olive Oyl, Brutus, Wimpy, Swee' Pea, Sultan, Wrestler. Synopsis: Popeye and Olive have a big fight and Popeye goes off and joins the Foreign Legion, while a sultan picks Olive to be his 75th wife.

Little Beau Pepé (Warner Bros., 1952) Title card

Legion Bound Hound. Hanna-Barbera Studios. Syndicated. Color. Air Date: September 17, 1960. 7mins. Producers/Directors: William Hanna, Joseph Barbera. Writer: Warren Foster. Animation: Kenneth Muse. Music: John Seeley. Layouts: Dick Reichenbach. Titles: Lawrence Goble. Cast: Huckleberry Hound, Powerful Pierre. Synopsis: Sgt. Hound is ordered to lead Company B to capture Powerful Pierre, but ends up going after the renegade alone.

Foreign Legion Leghorn. Warner Bros. ABC. Color. Air Date: April 19, 1962. Director: Robert McKimson. Writers: Friz Freleng and Chuck Jones. Animation: Motion Picture Screen Cartoonists Local 839. Cast: Foghorn Leghorn, Henery Hawk, Miss Prissy, Egghead, Jr. Synopsis: A soldier in the Foreign Legion, Foghorn, tells his sergeant his reasons for enlisting in the Legion during a desert trek.

Satiric Sands: Comedies and Cartoons

Legion Heirs. Hanna-Barbera Studios--Columbia Screen Gems. 5mins. Color. Air Date: April 1, 1963. Syndicated. Directors/Producers: Joseph Barbera, William Hanna. Animation: Kenneth Muse, Carlo Vinci, Dick Lundy. Voices: Daws Butler, Mel Blanc. Cast: Lippy the Lion, Hardy Har Har. Synopsis: Lippy and Hardy are drafted by the Foreign Legion to help rescue an admiral's daughter.

Heau Beau Jest. The Super 6 Show. DePatie-Freleng Enterprises. 10mins. Color. Air Date: November 19, 1966. NBC. Director: Steven Clark. Music: Bill Lava. Writer: Homer Brightman. Animation: Jim Davis. Cast: The Bros. Matzoriley, Siamese Triplets. Synopsis: In this segment of *The Super 6 Show* (oddly, the Bros. were not among that half dozen), the Bros. Matzoriley man a Legion fort which is singlehandedly besieged by Ali Ben Loudmouth.

Foreign Legion Flops. The Beagles Show. Total Television Prod./Leonardo TV Prod./Gamma Studios. Four parts, 5 minutes each. CBS. Air Dates: Part I--January 14, 1967. Pt. II--January 21, 1967. Pt. III--January 28, 1967. Pt. IV--February 4, 1967. Voices: Sandy Becker, Allan Swift, Kenny Delmar. Cast: Tubby, Stringer, Scotty.

Desert Knights. Hanna-Barbera. 5mins. Air Date: 1967. Cast: Laurel and Hardy. Synopsis: A young woman is held captive by a cruel Arab chieftain named Abba Ben Dabba.

Foreign Legion Droopy. Filmation Associates. Color. 7mins. Air Date: November 22, 1980. CBS-TV. Producers: Lou Scheimer, Norm Prescott. Voice: Frank Welker. Music: George Mahana. Cast: Droopy Dog, Slick the Wolf. Synopsis: Legionnaire Droopy is ordered to track down a wolf in sheik's clothing.

Foreign Legion Birds. Filmation Associates. Color. 7mins. Air Date: September 26, 1981. CBS. Animation: William Carney. Cast: Heckle and Jeckle.

Foreign Legion Air-Heads. Intermedia Entertainment/Marvel Prod. Ltd. Color. 30mins. Air Date: November 27, 1982. CBS. Producer: Bob Richardson. Voices: Ron Marak, Sally Julian, Frank Welker, Ronnie Schell. Music: Steven Depatie. Supervising Editor: Robert T. Gilles. Animation Directors: Gerry Chinquy, Tom Ray, John Gibbs. Cast: Meatballs, Spaghetti, Woofer, Clyde.

Foreign Legion Frenzy. Hanna-Barbera. Color. 5mins. Air Date: December 15, 1990. Fox. Director: Robert Alvarez. Producers: Joseph Barbera, Dun Jurwich. Writer: Dennis Marks. Voices: Don Messiah, Charlie Adler, Frank Welker. Animation Studio: Cuckoos Next Studios. Cast: Droopy Dog, Dripple, McWolf. Synopsis: McWolf single-handedly attempts to take a Legion fort defended by Droopy and Dripple.

Foreign Legion Gadget. DiC Entertainment. Color. 30mins. Air Date: October 12, 2003. Director: Bruno Bianchi. Writers: David Wiemers, Jean Chalpin, Ken Koonce, Kurt Weldon. Producer: Bruno Bianchi. Voices: Maurice LeMarche, Tegan Moss, Michael Dobson. Cast: Lt. Gadget, Col. Nosehair, Penny, R2K, Fidget, Digit. Synopsis: Lt. Gadget and Col Nosehair go on an undercover mission to capture a group of female criminals who were last seen near a French Foreign Legion encampment.

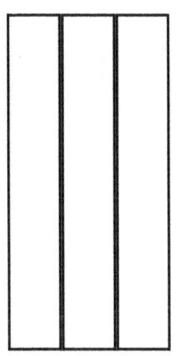

CHAPTER NINE
Sundry Sands:
The Legion on the Stage, Radio, and Television

As well as fighting in many nations of the world, the French Foreign Legion has been represented in all the other branches of the media beginning on the theatrical stage in the late nineteenth century.

Stage Productions

Under Two Flags

This seminal novel was extremely popular in the late nineteenth and early twentieth centuries as a subject for the stage. Besides the adaptations which were produced, there were a number of unproduced versions copyrighted from 1876 through 1914, including one entitled "Cigarette, or Under Two Flags" from 1883. There was even a satire in one act entitled "Under Two Jags" copyrighted by James Leonard in June 1914. This would not appear to be the basis for the Metro one-reel spoof filmed in 1923. (See Chapter 8.)

Under Two Flags
A play in 5 acts by C. H. Betts. Cincinnati, Ohio. October 28, 1876.

Under Two Flags
Dramatized by R. Ganthony in 11 scenes. October 19, 1885.

Under Two Flags
A. Mitchell, Arthur Williams. East London Theatre. A romantic play in 4 acts, dramatized from Ouida's famous novel. 1893.

Under Two Flags
David Belasco, adapted by Paul Potter, in partnership with Charles Frohman--Garden Theater, New York. February 5, 1901--c. June 1901. 135 performances. Five acts. Scenic Design: Ernest M. Gros. Cast: Blanche Bates, Francis Carlyle, Maclyn Arbuckle, Grace Elliston, Frank Leyden, Tefft Johnson, Arthur Bruce, Margaret Robinson, Matt Snyder, Rose Snyder, Edward S. Abeles, Albert Burning, Beresford Webb, Campbell Gollan, Madge West, William Sissons, Lem Roberts, Winchell B. Smith, Robert Tice, W. J. Welch, Malcolm Gunn, Arthur Benson, Mary Bayly.

New York Tribune, February 6, 1901: "Taste, thought, ingenuity and sedulous care were expended on every feature of the pageant...Every scene was a picture, every picture was harmonious with the place of the story to be illustrated...."

Under Two Flags
A romantic comedy drama in prologue and 3 acts by W. G. Browne. Chicago. August 12, 1901.

Under Two Flags
Paul Woodworth Hyde. 4 Acts. Pittsburgh. Opened October 14, 1901.

Under Two Flags
Princes Theatre, Bristol. June 4, 1903. Cast: Ida Molesworth, Alfred Hilliard.

Under Two Flags
Grand Theatre, Southampton. June 5, 1907. Adapted by Edward Elsrer. Cast: Charles Brooke, George Shaw, Wellesley Draper, Robert Faulkner, Michel Mannering.

Under Two Flags
Lyceum Theatre, London. March 10, 1908. The Potter version, presented by the Charles A. Taylor Company. Cast: Laurette Taylor. Special performance to raise money for a memorial fund for Ouida.

Under Two Flags
Grand Theatre, Southampton. June 28, 1909. Cast: Will Hook, Reginald Huntsworth, Mary Morrell, Daisy Carlton, Joseph Millane, Agnes Verity, Charles Brooke, George Shaw, Charles Johnson, Elizabeth Dundes, George Porteus, Francis Curtiss, Harry Pointy, Fred Clifford, William Beer, Stewart Enson, Alex Clayton, Joan Stern.

Under Two Flags
Theatre Royal, Exeter. 1915. Adaptation: Henrietta Schier. Cast: Hilary Burleigh, Eric Brighton.

Under Two Flags
Mark Blow. July 30, 1917.

Sundry Sands: The Legion on the Stage, Radio, and Television

Beau Geste

An immensely popular and influential novel (see Chapter 2), the quintessential French Foreign Legion story has proven less popular as a stage work.

Beau Geste

His Majesty's Theatre, London. Opened January 30, 1929. Produced by The Daniel Mayer Co.--Basil Dean and Alex L. Rea. Three acts. Stage Manager: A. L. Macleod. Orchestra Director: Albert Thompson. Stage Director: Thomas Warner. Set Designer: George W. Harris. Scenery Designer: Alick Johnstone. Cast: Laurence Olivier, Jack Hawkins, Robin Irvine, Edmund Wilard, Marie Lehr, Madeleine Carroll, Joan Henby, Clifton Boyne, Vincent Clive, Rose Austin, Mercia Gregori, Claude Horton, Ernest Wetherall, Reginald Arthur.

Laurence Olivier as Beau Geste

This production was strongly disliked by critics, who felt it was overly sentimental and written on a juvenile level. Opening night was disastrous, as the theatre fire warden overreacted to the "Viking funeral," in the final scene, bringing down the asbestos curtain rather noisily at the first sign of smoke. When it was again raised, the cast assembled on stage for a final bow to an empty house. The play ran only a month. Sir Laurence Olivier (1907-1989) was still at the beginning of his illustrious career, and would experience other setbacks before hitting his stride as the world's leading interpreter of Shakespeare. He would portray Beau Geste again on radio ten years later. (See under "Radio Productions.")

Scene from *Beau Geste* at His Majesty's Theatre

Der Legioner
By Lajos Biro. Apparently never produced, for this writer was unable to find any other data on it, except that it was written c. 1920 and served as the basis for a 1926 Hollywood film. (See Chapter 3.)

The Desert Song
Premiered November 30, 1926 at the Casino Theater, New York; ran through October 9, 1927, then moved to the Century Theatre and ran through November 1, 1927, before moving to the Imperial Theatre, where it ran from November 2, 1927, through January 7, 1928. An operetta in two acts and eight scenes. 471 performances. Book: Otto Harbach, Oscar Hammerstein II and Frank Mandel. Music: Sigmund Romberg. Libretto Direction: Arthur Hurley. Musical Numbers: Robert Connolly. Settings: Woodman Thompson. Producers:

Sundry Sands: The Legion on the Stage, Radio, and Television

Laurence Schwab and Frank Mandel. Cast: William O'Neal, O. J. Vanasse, Earl Mitchell, Eddie Buzzell, Glen Dale, Pearl Regay, Albert Baron, Charles Davis, Vivienne Segal, Edmund Elton, Robert Halliday, Nellie Breen, Elmira Lane, Lyle Evans, Margaret Irving, Rachel May Clark, Charles Morgan. *The Desert Song* was revived on Broadway in 1946, 1973 and 1987.

Ceux de la Legion
(Those of the Legion)

Operetta by Vincent Scotto. Premiered June 15, 1937, at the Theatre Antoine, Paris. Two acts. Book: Alibert, René Sarvil and Raymond Vinci. Songs: "Le souvenir de notre amour" ("The Remembrance of Our Love"), "Les Fortes Tetes" ("The Pigheaded Ones"). Music: Vincent Scotto. Lyrics: Raymond Vinci, René Sarvil, Ph. Loriol.

L'Enfant D'Obock
(The Child of Obock)

Play by Daniel Besnehard. Premiere March 8, 1994, at the Scene Nationale d'Aubusson. Three movements. Sets: Claire Chavanne. Costumes: Francoise Luro. Choreography: Christine Marneffe. Sound: Jacques Brault. Lighting: Pascal Murat. Cast: Francoise Bette, Yves Prunier, Cauthier Baillot, Gilles Dao, Karim Belkhadra, Jules-Emmanuel Eyoum Deido, Patrick Moutreuil. Synopsis: The wife of a legionnaire is bored at his new post in Djibouti and falls in love with a young Czech legionnaire.

Le Petit Maroc
(Little Morocco)

Play by Daniel Besnehard. Premiere July 24, 1998. Twelve scenes. Cast: Huguette Clery, Catherine Gandois, Gauthier Baillot. Synopsis: Two women are the wives of Legion officers at a post in the south of France. A young legionnaire arrives who is the nephew of one of the women and sleeps with the other.

Radio Productions

The Legionnaire and the Lady (*Morocco*). *Lux Radio Theatre*. CBS Network. Air Date: June 1, 1936. 60mins. Director: Frank Woodruff. Announcer: Melville Ruick. Adaptor: George Wells. Program Opening Announcer: Frank Nelson. With: Marlene Dietrich, Clark Gable, Frank Reichert, Walter Kingsford, Crauford Kent, James Eagles, Ynez Seabury, Karan Faris, Georges Renavent, Kenneth Hansen, Anne Stone, Margaret Brayton, Frank Nelson. This was the first *Lux Radio Theatre* broadcast from Hollywood.

Under Two Flags. *Lux Radio Theatre*. CBS Network. Air Date: May 31, 1937. 60mins. Director: Frank Woodruff. Adaptor: George Wells. Sound Effects: Charles Forsyth. Announcer: Melville Ruick. Music Director: Louis Silvers. Program Opening Announcer: Frank Nelson. With: Herbert Marshall, Olivia de Havilland, Lupe Velez, Louis Van Der Ecker, George Webb, Kenneth Hunter, Lal Chand Mehra, Leonard Mudie, Lionel Atwill, Lionel Pape, Lou Merrill.

Beau Geste. Campbell Playhouse. CBS Network. Air Date: March 17, 1939. 60mins. Announcer: Ernest Chappell. Narrator: Ray Collins. Composer and Conductor: Bernard Herrmann. Host: Orson Welles. With: Orson Welles, Laurence Olivier, Jackie Kelk, Noah Beery, Naomi Campbell, Edward Ryan, Stefan Schnabel, Elizabeth Elson, Kingsley Colton. A real legionnaire appeared as a guest, comparing the play with reality.

Beau Geste. Escape! CBS Network. Air Date: June 6, 1948. 30mins. Producer and Director: Norman MacDonnell. Adapted from the Wren novel by Les Crutchfield. Music: Lucien Moraweck. Conductor: Wilbur Hatch. Announcer: Roy Rowan. With: Jay Novello, Ben Wright, Lillian Buyeff, Peggy Webber, Barry Kroeger, Wilms Herbert, Ramsay Hill.

The Goon Show. BBC. Series 5, Episode 18--"Under Two Floorboards – A Story of the Legion." Air Date: January 25, 1955. 30mins. Writers: Spike Milligan, Eric Sykes. Announcer: Wallace "Bill" Greenslade. Producer: Peter Eton. Cast: Spike Milligan, Harry Secombe. Peter Sellers, Eccles, Bluebottle, Ray Ellington. Synopsis: Beau Geste is down from Cambridge when he attends a ball given by Lady Snowgoon. Her famous diamond, "The Blue Shower," is stolen from its display and Beau flees and joins the Foreign Legion.

Television Productions

Spike Jones and His Musical Depreciation Revue. Unaired Pilot. July 1950. 32mins. Sketch: "The Foreign Legion." 25mins. Producer: Jerry Fairbanks. Director: Eddie Cline. Writers: Eddie Maxwell, Eddie Brandt, Sol Meyer, Eddie Cline. Cast: Spike Jones, Billy Reed, Earl Bennett (Sir Fredrick Gas), Freddy Morgan, George Rock, Joe Siracusa, Dick Morgan, Bill King.

Colgate Comedy Hour. NBC. Air Date: September 16, 1951. 60mins. Sketch: "The Foreign Legion." 18mins. Producer: Ernie Gluckman. Writer: Jay Sommers. Cast: Spike Jones, Billy Reed, Earl Bennett, Freddy Morgan, George Rock, Joe Siracusa, Dick Morgan, Mac Pearson, Peter James, unidentified actress.

Douglas Fairbanks, Jr. Presents: The Foreign Legion. NBC. Dougfair Corp. United States/Great Britain. Air Date: 1952. Director: Daniel Birt. Director of Photography: Eric Cross. Screenplay: Anthony C. Bartley. Special Effects: Les Bowie, Val Elsey. Editor: Joseph Sterling. Asst. Editor: Peter Pitt. Art Directors: Les Bowie Burt Marshall, Val Elsey. Music: Ludo Phillip, Allan Gray. Producers: Anthony C. Bartley, Herman J. Blaser. Cast: Charles McGraw, Martin Benson, Mara Lane, Rufus Cruikshank, Ronan O'Casey, Oreste Orloff, Pepita Ramiriz, Gaston Riche, Lionel Grose, Michael Ritterman. Synopsis: A Legion patrol is attacked by a local tribe in the Sahara and one legionnaire is taken captive. A sergeant goes to rescue him and discovers that the daughter of another tribal chief is also a captive. Originally a pilot for a series, it was unsold and incorporated into this series.

Honneur et Fidelite (Honor and Loyalty). Air Date: 1952. French TV. Producer: Roger Blanc. A documentary giving the Legion's history, from the war in Mexico to the war in Indochina.

Sundry Sands: The Legion on the Stage, Radio, and Television

The Spike Jones Show. NBC. 30mins. Air Date: March 6, 1954. Producer: Ed Sobel. Director: Bud Yorkin. Writers: Freddie Morgan, Sol Meyer, Eddie Maxwell, Eddie Brandt. Sketch: "The Foreign Legion." 20mins. Cast: Spike Jones, Freddy Morgan, George Rock, Mac Pearson, Bernie Jones, Helen Grayco, Peter James, Earl Bennett, Billy Barty.

Captain Gallant of the Foreign Legion. NBC. February 13, 1955–March 24, 1957. ABC. June 6, 1960-January 2, 1961 (reruns). *Foreign Legionnaire* (NBC and syndicated) September 21, 1963 (reruns). 30mins. Producer: Gilbert A. Ralston. Music: Guy Luypaerts. Regular Cast: Buster Crabbe, Cullen Crabbe, Fuzzy Knight, Giles Queant, Norma Eberhardt, Roger Trenielle, Daniel Lecourtois.

The first season was filmed in a town called Zagora in Morocco at a real Foreign Legion outpost. Actual legionnaires and local Arabs were used as extras. Interiors were shot at studios in Paris and Rome. The second season was filmed in Tirrenia in Italy with Italian actors standing in for Arabs. Buster Crabbe, in the title role of Capt. Michael Gallant, received $1,000 per episode plus a percentage of the profits.

Episodes—First Season

1. *Introduction* — Air Date: February 13, 1955
2. *Veils of Death* — Air Date: February 20, 1955
3. *Firepower* — Air Date: February 27, 1955
4. *Tala's Secret* — Air Date: March 6, 1955
5. *The Camel Race* — Air Date: March 13, 1955
6. *Esprit de Corps* — Air Date: March 20, 1955
7. *Carnival in Zagora* — Air Date: March 27, 1955
8. *Twenty Fathoms Under the Desert* — Air Date: April 3, 1955
9. *Strange Sanctuary* — Air Date: April 10, 1955
10. *The Prayer Rug* — Air Date: April 17, 1955
11. *The Golden Loop* — Air Date: April 24, 1955
12. *Caravan Patrol* — Air Date: May 1, 1955
13. *Tina* — Air Date: May 8, 1955
14. *The Captive Oasis* — Air Date: May 15, 1955
15. *Revenge* — Air Date: May 22, 1955
16. *As Long As There Will Be Money* — Air Date: May 29, 1955
17. *Ambushed* — Air Date: June 5, 1955
18. *The Jewel Box* — Air Date: June 12, 1955
19. *The Man with the Mat* — Air Date: June 19, 1955
20. *The Dagger of Judith* — Air Date: June 26, 1955
21. *The Lady from Zagora* — Air Date: September 11, 1955
22. *Pipeline* — Air Date: September 18, 1955
23. *Double Jeopardy* — Air Date: September 25, 1955
24. *Desert Justice* — Air Date: October 2, 1955
25. *Treasure of the Legion* — Air Date: October 9, 1955
26. *The Hostage* — Air Date: October 16, 1955
27. *Ransom* — Air Date: October 23, 1955

28. *The Legion Is Our Home*　　　　Air Date: October 30, 1955
29. *The Traitor*　　　　Air Date: November 6, 1955
30. *The Hand of Fatima*　　　　Air Date: November 13, 1955
31. *The Hat*　　　　Air Date: November 20, 1955
32. *Alibi*　　　　Air Date: November 27, 1955
33. *The Lost Caravan*　　　　Air Date: December 4, 1955
34. *Masquerade*　　　　Air Date: December 11, 1955
35. *The Clue of Herodotus*　　　　Air Date: December 18, 1955
36. *The Little Boy Who Found Christmas*　　　　Air Date: December 25, 1955
37. *The Constance Missal*　　　　Air Date: January 2, 1956

Episodes—Second Season

1. *Gallant's New Post*　　　　Air Date: September 16, 1956
2. *Cuffy's Guides*　　　　Air Date: September 23, 1956
3. *The Long Night*　　　　Air Date: September 30, 1956
4. *Cuffy's Present*　　　　Air Date: October 7, 1956
5. *The Flaming Hoop*　　　　Air Date: October 14, 1956
6. *Rodeo*　　　　Air Date: October 21, 1956
7. *Fuzzy's Furlough*　　　　Air Date: October 28, 1956
8. *The Magic Lamp*　　　　Air Date: November 4, 1956
9. *A Private Affair*　　　　Air Date: November 11, 1955
10. *The Informer's Map*　　　　Air Date: November 18, 1956
11. *Cuffy's Good Deed*　　　　Air Date: November 25, 1956
12. *Guns for Sale*　　　　Air Date: December 2, 1956
13. *Shifting Sands*　　　　Air Date: December 9, 1956
14. *The Sword of El Kiri*　　　　Air Date: December 16, 1956
15. *Mystery Man of the Desert*　　　　Air Date: January 6, 1957
16. *Out of Bounds*　　　　Air Date: January 13, 1957
17. *Water*　　　　Air Date: January 20, 1957
18. *Ring of Steel*　　　　Air Date: January 27, 1957
19. *The Third Person*　　　　Air Date: February 3, 1957
20. *One Accident Too Many*　　　　Air Date: February 10, 1957
21. *Dr. Legionnaire*　　　　Air Date: February 17, 1957
22. *Rescue*　　　　Air Date: February 24, 1957
23. *Lone Legionnaire*　　　　Air Date: March 3, 1957
24. *Court Martial*　　　　Air Date: March 10, 1957
25. *The Man from Cairo*　　　　Air Date: March 17, 1957
26. *Too Many Suspects*　　　　Air Date: March 24, 1957

The Desert Song. NBC. 90mins. Color. Air Date: May 7, 1955. Producer: Max Lieberman. Writers: William Friedberg, Will Glickman. Cast: Nelson Eddy, Gale Sherwood, Otto Kruger, Viola Essen, John Conte, Earl William, Salvatore Baccalon. The original color version no longer exists; only a black-and-white print is available.

Sundry Sands: The Legion on the Stage, Radio, and Television

Captain Gallant of the Foreign Legion (NBC-TV, 1955-57) Buster and Cullen Crabbe

The Desert Song (NBC-TV, 1955) Gale Sherwood and Nelson Eddy

Sundry Sands: The Legion on the Stage, Radio, and Television

Soldiers of Fortune. Syndicated. 30mins. Air Date: January 13, 1957. *Attack at Ras Al Ma.* Director: Richard Irving. Writer: Fenton Earnshaw. Photography: Ellis Thackery, A.S.C. Editor: Edward Hare   Editorial Supervisor: Richard G. Wray, A.C.E. Art Director: George Patrick. Asst. Director: James Nicholson. Set Decoration: Howard Walker. Music Supervision: Stanley Wilson. Costume Supervisor: Vincent Dee. Cast: John Russell, Chick Chandler, Ted De Corsia, Suzanne Cummings, George Baxter, Nico Minardos, Byron Palmer. Synopsis: In Algeria, Tim Kelly and Toubo Smith come upon a Foreign Legion patrol under attack by Arabs. They climb a ridge behind the Arabs and drive them off. The sergeant is an old friend of theirs and they return with him to Sidi-Bel-Abbes. The commanding officer there learns the two were guests of an Arab chieftain and asks for information about his movements. Learning that he plans to attack Ras Al Ma, he prepares his troops to march to the aid of that city. Meanwhile, the commanding officer's daughter is seeing the chieftain's son. A legionnaire sees them in a tavern and makes a scene. He is later murdered in an alley. The daughter is kidnapped by the chieftain and Kelly and Smith join the Legion to lead some volunteers to rescue her. They succeed and discover a loophole which lets them leave the Legion. Footage from *Outpost in Morocco* (1949) [q.v.] was used in the action scenes.

Soldiers of Fortune. Syndicated. 30mins. Air Date: January 20, 1957. *Guns for El Khadar.* Director: Richard Irving. Story and Teleplay: Fenton Earnshaw. Original Music: Paul Dunlap. Cast: John Russell, Chick Chandler, George Baxter, Jean Del Val, John Doucette, Austin Green, Walter Kray, Edward Manouk, Lee Van Cleef. Synopsis: Someone is supplying arms to Arab tribesmen to use against the French Foreign Legion. Tim Kelly and Toubo Smith help some legionnaires in finding them.

The Spike Jones Show. CBS. 30mins. Air Date: April 30, 1957. Sketch: "The Foreign Legion." 10mins. Producers: Dik Darley and Tom Waldman. Directors: Tom Waldman and Dik Darley. Writers: Tom Waldman, Danny Arnold, Eddie Brandt. Cast: Nelson Eddy, Spike Jones, Freddy Morgan, Mousie Garner, Jad Paul, Phil Gray, Eddie Robertson, Billy Barty.

Assignment Foreign Legion. Syndicated. 1956-1957. 30mins. Producers: E.M. Smedley Aston and Anthony Bartley/Intel Films for CBS Films. Narration: Merle Oberon (1911-1979), who played a foreign correspondent stationed in North Africa; she also appeared in some episodes. September 1956 British premiere--26 episodes. September 1957 American premiere--13 episodes. Anthology --Dramatizations based on the role of the French Foreign Legion during the North African campaign in World War II. Such well-known actors as Lionel Jeffries, Christopher Lee and Martin Benson appeared in some episodes. Partly shot on location in Algeria and Morocco and at Beaconsfield Studios.

British Episodes:

1. *The Stripes of Sgt. Schweiger*	Air Date: September 21, 1956
2. *The Baroness*	Air Date: September 28, 1956
3. *The Man Who Found Freedom*	Air Date: October 5, 1956
4. *The Search*	Air Date: October 12, 1956
5. *The Thin Line*	Air Date: October 18, 1956
6. *The Glory That Was Meister*	Air Date: October 26, 1956

7. *The Stool Pigeon* — Air Date: November 2, 1956
8. *The Ghost* — Air Date: November 9, 1956
9. *Finger Your Neck* — Air Date: November 16, 1956
10. *The Outcast* — Air Date: November 23, 1956
11. *Dollar a Year Man* — Air Date: November 30, 1956
12. *The Anaya* — Air Date: December 7, 1956
13. *Sword of Truth* — Air Date: December 14, 1956
14. *A Matter of Honour* — Air Date: December 21, 1956
15. *The Debt* — Air Date: December 28, 1956
16. *The White Kepi* — Air Date: January 4, 1957
17. *Testimonial to a Soldier* — Air Date: January 11, 1957
18. *A Pony for Joe Crazy Horse* — Air Date: January 18, 1957
19. *The Conquering Hero* — Air Date: January 25, 1957
20. *As We Forgive* — Air Date: February 1, 1957 164
21. *The Richest Man in the Legion* — Air Date: February 8, 1957
22. *The Deserter* — Air Date: February 15, 1957
23. *The Coward* — Air Date: February 22, 1957
24. *Mixed Blood* — Air Date: March 1, 1957
25. *The White Witch of Makala* — Air Date: March 8, 1957
26. *The Volunteer* — Air Date: March 15, 1957

American Episodes:

1. *The Outcast* — Air Date: October 1, 1957
2. *The Ghost* — Air Date: October 8, 1957
3. *The White Kepi* — Air Date: October 15, 1957
4. *The Stripes of Sergeant Schweiger* — Air Date: October 22, 1957
5. *The Debt* — Air Date: October 29, 1957
6. *A Matter of Honor* — Air Date: November 5, 1957
7. *The Man Who Found Freedom* — Air Date: November 12, 1957
8. *A Pony for Joe Crazy Horse* — Air Date: November 19, 1957
9. *The Stool Pigeon* — Air Date: November 26, 1957
10. *The Thin Line* — Air Date: December 3, 1957
11. *The Testimonial of a Soldier* — Air Date: December 17, 1957
12. *The Anaya* — Air Date: December 24, 1957
13. *As We Forgive* — Air Date: March 11, 1958 165

Der Fall Kapitan Behrens--Fremdenlegionare an Bord (The Case of Captain Behrens--Legionnaires on Board) Aurora Television Prod. GmbH (Hamburg) in association with Zweites Deutsches Fernsehen. (ZDF). (Mainz, Germany). Air Date: February 4, 1966. 72mins. Director: Wolfgang Staudte. Teleplay: Gunther Wolf, Peter Ernst. Art Direction: Gunther Kob. Cast: Wolfgang Preiss, Hans Schellbach, Manfred Reddemann, Jochan Sehrndt, Peter Heusch, Fritz Suppan, Harald Eggers, Willem Fricke, Jurgen Dieckmann, Franz Rudnick, Jurgen Janza, Edgar Frank, Frank Straas, Heinz Piper, Narziss Sokatscheff, Raymond Joob, Peter Frank, Jons Andersson, Victor Warsitz, Marquard Bohm.

Sundry Sands: The Legion on the Stage, Radio, and Television

The Man from U.N.C.L.E. NBC. Air Date: February 18, 1966. 60mins. *The Foreign Legion Affair*. Executive Producer: Norman Felton. Director: John Brahm. Music: Jerry Goldsmith. Story: Berne Giler. Cast: Robert Vaughn, David McCallum, Leo G. Carroll, Howard Da Silva, Danielle DeMetz. Synopsis: Illya parachutes from a plane with THRUSH code documents. He lands in an abandoned French Foreign Legion fort run by Capt. Basil Calhoun. He is accompanied by a stewardess named Barbara. Napoleon Solo rushes to save them before THRUSH finds them.

End of an Empire. MacMillan Films, United States. 1968. CBS. 26mins. Black and White. Documentary about France's Indo-Chinese War.

Man Alive: The French Foreign Legion, Beau Geste--And Since. BBC. Great Britain. 1971. Director: Harry Weisbloom. Editors: Desmond Wilcox, Bill Morton. Reporter: D. Wilcox. An examination of Legion traditions and present-day training methods.

La Legion Etrangere (*The Foreign Legion*). Canadian Broadcasting Co. 60mins. Air Date: October 1972. Producer-Director: Robert D. Clarke. Writer: Peter Ward. Narrator: Bill Kehoe. Cameramen: Ian Matheson and Guy Weese. A documentary about the modern Legion, which portrays the day-to-day life of the legionnaires, it features interviews with historians and veterans added to sequences showing the lifestyle of the modern legionnaire. To get permission to film this project, the CBC crew members had to agree to keep up with the soldiers' regimen.

Les Douze Legionnaires (*Twelve Legionnaires*). Antenne 2. (France). Air Date: August 2, 1976. Thirteen episodes, 26 minutes each. Director: Bernard Borderie. Script: Bernard Borderie, Paul Bonnecarrére. Cast: Yves Vincent, Pierre Londiche, Jacques Bonnevarrére, Francis Roure, Henri Czarniak, Philippe Paulino, Nathalie Drivet, André Batisse, Richard Martin, Jean Toscan, Daniel Perche, Philip Lemaire, Pierre Hatet, Maurice Biraud, Jean Claudio.

1. *Italy*
2. *Germany*
3. *Indochina*
4. *Tonkin Delta*
5. *Namh-Dinh, Master Sergeant Ky Vanost*
6. Cao Bang, Indochina: Master Sergeant Steine, Master Sergeant Kloff
7. Algeria: Master Sergeant Hans Müller
8. Ouarsenis: Master Sergeant Jacques Larue
9. Sahara: Master Sergeant Sevek
10. *Calvi: Corporal maggiore Prude*
11. *Il Tenente*
12. *The Final Command*
13. Attack

60 Minutes. CBS. Air Date: 1979. *The Foreign Legion*.

Le Main Coupée (*The Cut Hand*). French TV. Air Date: September 20, 1979. Director: Jean Kerchbron. Screenplay: J. Kerchbron, from the novel by Blaise Cendrars. Photography: Jean Graglia, Bernard Auronet, Roger Wrona. Music: Francis Lemarque. Cast: Patrick Préjean, Stephane Shandor, Maurice Paquot, Pierre Chevalier, Pierre Baton, Jean Franval, Sady Rebbot, Xavier Van Den Bergh, Jean Kuisi, Jean Pierre Zola, Jacques Mauclair, Andre Cellier, Jean Tolzac, Michel Morano, Rico Lopez, Gino Da Ronch, Daniel Verité. Recounts the experiences of Blaise Cendrars in the Legion from 1914-1918.

Des Hommes Sans Nom (*Men Without A Name*). French TV TF1. Air Date: December 11, 1979. Producers: Jean-Francois Chauvel and Anne de Boismilon. Documentary.

Beau Geste. Great Britain, 1982. BBC TV mini-series. Eight episodes, transmitted on BBC1, each episode 30 minutes. Director: Douglas Camfield. Producer: Barry Letts. Writer: Alistair Bell, based on the novel by P. C. Wren. Photography: Trevor Wimlett, Chris Wickham. Music Composer/Conductor: Stephen Deutsch. Costumes: Catriona Tomalin. Makeup: Jan Wethercot. Script Editor: Terrance Dicks. Production Asst.: Eileen Staff. Production Manager: Ann Aronsohn. Military Advisor: Martin Windrow. Lighting: John Mason.

Episode 1 Air Date: October 31, 1982
Episode 2 Air Date: November 7, 1982
Episode 3 Air Date: November 14, 1982
Episode 4 Air Date: November 21, 1982
Episode 5 Air Date: November 28, 1982
Episode 6 Air Date: December 5, 1982
Episode 7 Air Date: December 12, 1982
Episode 8: Air Date: December 19, 1982

Cast: Benedict Taylor, Anthony Calf, Jonathon Morris, John Forgeham, Stefan Gryff, Sally Baxter, Wendy Williams, David Sumner, Christopher Malcolm, Barry Dennen, Paul Hawkins, Paul Critchley, Robin Crane, David Shawyer, Damien Thomas, Bunny Reed, John Moreno, John Patrick, Kenneth Owens, Terry Raven, Nicolas Chagrin, Randal Herley, Andrew Armour, Nadio Fortune, Terry Gurry, Philip Shelley, John Challis, Christopher Reilly, John Repsch, Jon Rumney, Robert Vowles, Jonathan Bum, Maurice Quick, Red Milner, Daniel André Pageon, Barry Summerford, John Cannon, Harry Fielder, Pat Gorman, Les Conrad, Julia Chambers, Andrew Lodge, Lucy Baker.

Legion, Dernier Far West. 1980s. Documentary shot with the collaboration of the French Foreign Legion.

The French Foreign Legion. Network TV in association with the BBC. Great Britain. 1983. Director: Michael Frewin. Producer: Jeremy Hunter. Script: J. Hunter. Photography: Michael Miles. Editor: Richard Seel. Presenter: Simon Murray. Murray, an ex-legionnaire, contrasts the public perception of the Foreign Legion with film clips of the present Legion.

Beau Geste (BBC-TV, 1982) The burning of Fort Zinderneuf

3-2-1: The French Foreign Legion. Yorkshire Television. Great Britain. Air Date: March 19, 1983. Executive Producer: Alan Tarrant. Director: Don Clayton. Producer: Ian Bolt. Compiler: Deborah Sutherland. Researcher: Shirley Jones. Script: John Bartlett, Wally Malston. Designer: David Crozier. Music Direction: Laurie Holloway. Host: Ted Rogers. Cast: Chris Emmett, Mike Newman, Christopher Beeny, Dilys Watling, Caroline Munro, Felix Bowness.

Il Segreto Del Sahara (*The Secret of the Sahara*). Raiuno/Beta Film/ ZDF/TVE/Racing Pictures/Artisti Associati. Italy. Air Date: January 3, 1988. Mini-series in four parts. Color. 360mins. Director: Alberto Negrin. Producer: Alessandro Fracassi. Screenplay: A. Negrin, Nicola Badalucco, Sergio Donati. Story: Nicola Badalucco, Massimo De Rita, Sergio Donati, Lucio Mandara, from the novel by Emilio Salgari. Photography: Daniele Nannuzzi. Music: Ennio Morricone. Art Director: Francesca Lo Schiavo. Costumes: Alberto Verso. Editor: Mario Morra. Production Design: Dante Ferretti. Cast: Michael York, Ben Kingsley, Andie McDowell, David Soul, Miguel Bose, Mathilda May, William McNamara, Diego

Abatantuono, Jean Pierre Cassel, James Farentino. Synopsis: An archaeologist discovers an old parchment which mentions a fabulous treasure buried somewhere in "Loudspeaker Mountain." A legionnaire officer, his men and a desert bandit also become involved in the search.

Beau Geste (BBC TV, 1982) Jonathan Morris, Benedict Taylor and Anthony Calf

Die Legion Ist Unser Vaterland--Geschichte Einer Legendarischen Truppe (The Legion is Our Fatherland--Story of a Legendary Corps). Germany. 1988. 45mins. Director: William Reschl. Documentary on the Legion's history.

La Legion. French TV. TF1. Air Date: February 22, 1990. Producer: Pierre Schoendoerffer. Documentary.

Ma Legion (My Legion). France. Channel FR3. Air Date: February 25, 1991. Producers: Martin Ledniczky, Csaba Kardos and Ferenc Darvas. Documentary, part of the series *Oceaniques*, an abridged version of the 1989 Hungarian film of the same title (see Chapter 7).

World of Valor. Discovery Channel in association with 44 Blue Prod. United States. Air Date: November 5, 1992. Documentary about the modern Legion.

Muukalaislegioonalainen 97297. Yleisradio (YLE). Finnish TV. 45mins. Air Date: March 31, 1993. Director: Tapani Itaranta. Screenplay: T. Itaranta. Cast: Leo Vikki.

La Legion Etrangére (The Foreign Legion). French TV. TF1. Air Date: July 11, 1994. Producer: Patrick Jeudy. A documentary, part of the TV series *Les Fabuleuses Archives de L'armée Francaise (The Fabulous Archives of the French Army)*.

Sundry Sands: The Legion on the Stage, Radio, and Television

La Legion: Les Hommes Sans Nom (The Legion, Men Without Names). France. TF 1. Air Date: February 8, 1995. Producers: Charles Villeneuve and Gerard David. Documentary, part of the series *Le Droit de Savior*.

La Legion Est Notre Patrie: Histoire et Legende (The Legion is Our Fatherland: History and Legend). France-Germany. Arte Channel. Air Date: June 11, 1995. Producer: Wilhelm Reschl.

Paroles de Legion (Legion's Words). France. 1995. 45mins. Director: Martine Jouando. Interviews with real legionnaires and officers.

Foreign Legion--Part 1. Ecosse Films, Scotland. Channel 4. 1996. *Men With No Name--The Recruit*. Director: Ian Taylor. Producer: Douglas Rae. Asst. Producer: Jerry Hunter. Production Managers: Emma Crawford, Lucy Currie. Photography: Paul Otter. Special Effects: Molinare. Editor: Noel Chanan. Sound: Mark Hatch. Synopsis: A young former Royal Marine enlists in the Foreign Legion in Paris, and then travels to Aubagne to go through some very tough training.

Foreign Legion--Part 2. Ecosse Films, Scotland. Channel 4. 1996. *Men With No Name--Jungle Warriors*. Director: Ian Taylor. Producer: Douglas Rae. Asst. Producer: Jeremy Hunter. Production Managers: Emma Crawford, Lucy Currie. Photography: Paul Otter. Special Effects: Molinare. Editor: Noel Chanan. Sound: Mark Hatch. Synopsis: Legion trainees are sent on active service to French Guyana, where they endure thirty days of intense exercises in bad weather.

Un Homme D'Honneur: Le Second Proces D'Helie de Saint-Marc (A Man of Honor: Helie de Saint-Marc's Second Trial). France. Air Date: February 23, 1997. Producers: Patrick Jeudy and Laurent Beccaria. Episode of the TV series *Le Sens de l'Histoire (The Sense of History)*. Saint-Marc is a renowned ex-officer of the Legion who switched to the OAS during the Algerian War.

Die Fremdenlegion (The Foreign Legion). Germany. 1997. Director: Jacek Blawut. Producer: Ilone Ziok. Documentary.

Warriors of the French Foreign Legion. United States. National Geographic /Discovery Channel, in association with Magna Pacific. 50mins. Air Date: 2000. Director: Mark Hillier. Writer: Michael Schlossman. Documentary about the modern Legion.

Fremmedlegionaeren (The French Foreign Legionnaire). Nordisk Film. Norway. Air Date: March 1, 2001. 25mins. Director and Writer: Elisabeth Nord. Documentary short about a twenty-one-year-old Norwegian looking for adventure who joins the French Foreign Legion.

Legio Patria Nostra (The Legion, Our Country) aka *Het, Legionen is ons vaderland (The Legion is our Fatherland)*. The Netherlands. Air Date: September 30, 2001. 58mins. Directors: Naarten Schmidt and Thomas Doebele. Documentary about the modern Legion.

Le Droit De Savoir (The Right to Know). France 2001--TAP/Comiti Prod. Series. French Foreign Legion episode: *Les Missions Impossible Hommes Sans Nom (Legion: Impossible Missions of Men Without a Name)*. Director: Oliver Santicchi. Photography: Lionel Audibert. Editor: Tony Meyer.

Legion: Des Hommes Sans Nom (The Legion: Men Without a Name.) France 2002--France 2. Director: Jean-Baptiste Gallot. Documentary on the current Legion in the Ivory Coast, Djibouti and French Guiana.

Des Hommes Sans Passe (Men Without a Past). France. 2003--TAP/Comiti Prod. 70mins. Director: Jean Baptiste Gallot. Photography: J. B. Gallot, Christophe Fonseca. Editor: Fabien Galliufo. Narrator: Anotione Gueland. Sound: Michel Cailly. Another documentary entry in the *Le Droit De Savoir* series. A group of legionnaires is shown on a mission against rebels in the Ivory Coast. Training periods in Djibouti and French Guyana are also shown.

In Fremden Diensten Deutsche Legionare Im Indochinakrieg (In Foreign Services--German Legionnaires in The Indochina War). Germany. Air Date: February 9, 2004. 52mins. Director: Marc Eberle. Story: Thomas Tilsch. Photography: Richard Laokani. Editors: Michele Barbin, Alex Feil. Music: Nils Kacirek. Producers: Annette Fuss for Filmtank (Hamburg) and Bayrischer Rundfunk (Bavarian Radio). A mixture of newsreels and talking heads about the involvement of German legionnaires in Indochina; apparently, 70% of the legionnaires fighting there were either of German or Austrian descent. They had been recruited from refugee camps or Prisoner of War camps, many of them housing SS which only a couple of years before fought France. The legionnaires identified are Gunther Woizik, Eugen Brause, Joachim Schriever, Willy Deckers and Heinrich Kleinholz. A large number of them (1,400), after a while, deserted to the Viet-Minh and fought with them. Many later returned as heroes to the German Democratic Republic, which tried then to recruit them as spies for the Cold War.

Dien Bien Phu: Le Rapport Secret. France. Point Du Jour/France 3. Color. Air Date: May 6, 2004. 57mins. Director: Patrick Jeudy. Script: P. Jeudy. Cinematography: Stéphane Saporito, Igor Ochronowitz. Editor: Barthélémy Vieillot. Sound: Guy Robertson Rabanrivello. Documentary about the battle that drove the French from Indo-China (Vietnam).

Les Recrues de la Seconde Chance (Second Chance Recruits). France 2005--TAP/Comiti Prod. 75mins. Directors: Philippe Bodet and Jean-Pierre Guillerez. Photography: J. Guillerez. Producer: Tony Comiti. Editor: Anne Marty. Music: Thomas Dappelo. Sound: Michel Cailly. Another entry in the *Le Droit de Savoir* series. A group of trainees are followed from their first day until they become full-fledged legionnaires. Shot mainly in France and French Guyana.

Je Serai Legionnaire (I Will Be a Legionnaire). France. Channel 5. 2005. 52mins. Director: Pierre Henry-Mentheour. Narrator: Bernard Laine. Documentary about the induction of three young legionnaires.

Immersion Totales La Legion Etrangere (Complete Immersion into the Foreign Legion). Second Channel (France). Air Date: July 6, 2006. 90mins. Director: Frederique Oger.

Sundry Sands: The Legion on the Stage, Radio, and Television

Narration: Carol Gaessler. Writer: Frederique Lacroix. Editor: Frederique Oger. Producer: Vincent Dhennim. Documentary about modern legionnaires from basic training to the civil war in the Ivory Coast.

Au Coeur De La Legion- Des Hommes des Exception (*In the Heart of the Legion--Exceptional Men*). Channel 5--C Productions. (France). Air Date: October 2006. 100mins. Director: Bruno Evenou. Writers: Jean Marc Tricaud, Valerie Troisier and Melissa Theuriau. Editor: Vincent Evrard. Photography: Eric Mappi, Christophe Garcia, Philippe Chatot, Damien Augeroles, Hervé Schwerdel, Ivan Bodineau. Part of a documentary series entitled *Zone Interdite* (*Forbidden Zone*).

The French Foreign Legion: Tougher Than the Rest. ITV4. Great Britain. Air Date: October 10, 2007. 47mins. Creator: Elisabeth Nord. Writer: Vibeke Strøm. Executive Producers: E. Nord. V. Strøm. Cinematography: Elisabeth Nord. Editor: Geraint Huw Reynolds. Documentary portraying daily life in the current Legion.

§

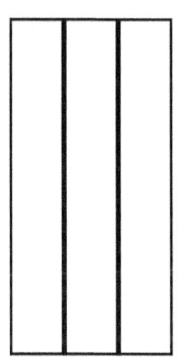

CHAPTER TEN
Superfluous Sands: Marginal French Foreign Legion Films and Spanish Foreign Legion Films

As with most film sub-genres, there are productions which only contain minor elements relating to that genre. Such is the case with French Foreign Legion films; in fact, such marginal films are, if you will excuse the pun, legion. A number of motion pictures feature minor characters who are or were legionnaires, mention the Legion, or have but one or two scenes concerned with the Legion. The following list may not be complete, but gives the reader some idea of the extent of the French Foreign Legion's popularity as a film subject.

Films about the *Chasseurs d'Afrique*: All five silent versions of *Under Two Flags* were about the *Chasseurs d'Afrique*, as in the novel (see Chapter 1).

Marginal French Foreign Legion Films:

The Jewels of Allah (Thanhouser, USA, 1911)
L'Atlantide (International et Commercial de Cinematographie/Societé General pour le Developpement, France, 1921)
The Truants (Stoll, GB, 1922)
Gigolo (PDC/DeMille, USA, 1926)
Hangman's House (Fox, USA, 1928)
Gantsirulni (aka Doomed) (Sakhkinmretsvi, USSR, 1930)
Die Herrin von Atlantis (aka *The Mistress of Atlantis*) (Nero-Film AG, Germany, 1932)
Le Prince Jean (Fox, France, 1934)
The World Moves On (Fox, USA, 1934)
Valborgsmassoafton (Walpurgisnight) (Sweden, 1935)
The Garden of Allah (Selznick, USA, 1936)
Les Reprouvés (Hades Film, France, 1936)
Pilot X (Puritan Pictures, USA, 1937)

Have You Any Castles? (Warner Bros. cartoon, USA, 1938)
Livet Gar Vidare (Life Goes On) (Sweden, 1941)
Caballeria del imperio (*The King's Horsemen*) (Mexico, 1942)
Mexicanos al grito de guerra (*Historia del Himno Nacional*) (Mexico, 1943)
Night and Day (Warner Bros., USA, 1946)
Les demons de L'aube (*Demons of Dawn*) (Gaumont, France, 1946)
Siren of Atlantis (aka *Atlantis, the Lost Continent*) (United Artists, USA, 1949)
Kyssen Po Kryssen (Saga Films, Sweden, 1950)
Toto Sceicco (Toto the Sheik) (Manenti Film Sp. A., 1950)
Meet Me After The Show (20th Century-Fox, USA, 1951)
Operation Secret (Warner Bros., USA, 1952)
Les Belles de Nuit (Franco-London Films, France, 1952)
Dreamboat (20th Century-Fox, USA, 1952)
A Day to Remember (GFD, Great Britain, 1953)
Alerte Au Sud (*Alert in the South*) (Fono Roma/Neptune/Sirius Italy-France, 1953)
Komm Zuruck (*Come Back*) (Divana-Film GmbH, Germany, 1953)
Donald's Diary (Walt Disney/RKO cartoon, 1954)
The Sad Sack (Paramount, USA, 1957)
Senechal le Magnifique (*Senechal the Magnificent*)(Chronos-Ucil-Cinedis, France, 1957)
Border Affair (U.S. TV, episode of *Cheyenne,* 1957)
Ascenseur pour Lechafaud (*Elevator to the Gallows*; U.S.: *Frantic*) Nouvelles Editions de Films, France, 1958)
Lafayette Escadrille (Warner Bros., USA, 1958)
Soldaterkammarater (*Comrades in Arms*) (Denmark, 1958)
Le Sahara Brule (*Sahara on Fire*; US: *Flame in the Desert*) (France, 1961)
Jules Verne (Peabody and Sherman cartoon, Jay Ward, USA, 1962)
Dragées Au Poivre (*Peppery Sweets*) (Dicifrance, France, 1963)
The Brides of Fu Manchu (Fu Manchu/Seven Arts/Constantin, Great Britain, 1966)
Objectif 500 Millions (Société Nouvelle de Cinematographie/Rome-Paris Film, France, 1966)
The Monkees (US TV, band dressed as legionnaires while singing "Tomorrow's Another Day", 1966)
Casino Royale (Columbia-Ceiad, Great Britain, 1967)
Adieu L'Ami (*Farewell, Friend*) (Greenwich Film Prod., France, 1968; U.S.: 1973)
Le Dernier Saut (*The Last Leap*) (CFDC/FidaCinematografica/Lira Films/Pathé/ Sonocam/ UGC Images, Italy- France, 1969)
Emitai (*Thunder God*) (Filmi Domirev, Senegal, 1971)
L'Atlantide (French TV, 1972) Legion (French TV, 1972)
La Cagna (*The Bitch*) (Lira Films/Pathé, France/Italy, 1972)
Der Haendler der Vier Jahreszeiten (*The Merchant of Four Seasons*) (Tango Film, Germany, 1972)
Paul Lynde Halloween Special (ABC-TV, U.S., 1976)
Those Lips, Those Eyes (United Artists, USA, 1980)
Le Grand Frere (*Big Brother*) (TP1 Films/SFPC Odena Films, France, 1982)
Le Matelot 512 (*Able Seaman #512*) (Centre Mediterrannéen de Creation Cinematographique, France, 1984)

SUPERFLUOUS SANDS: MARGINAL FRENCH AND SPANISH FOREIGN LEGION FILMS

Oceano (Italian-Spanish TV, 1989)
It Ain't Necessarily So (U.S. TV, episode of *Jake and the Fatman*, 1989)
Lionheart (Guild/Imperial/Suniel/Wrong Bet Prod., USA, 1990)
*Le Gorille Compte Ses Abati*s (French TV, 1990, episode in series *Le Gorille*)
Camerone (German TV, 1992, episode #254 in series *Tatort* (*Crime Scene*)
L'Atlantide (Aura Film, France, 1992)
Cecile est Morte (*Cecile is Dead*) (French TV, episode in *Maigret* series 1994)
Le Vent Du Wyoming (*The Wind of Wyoming*) (Eiffel/Les Prod. EGM/Transfilm, France, 1994)
Le Rocher d'Acapulco (*Acapulco Rock*) (Elison/F.R.P./Key Light, France, 1996)
Savior (Lions Gate, USA, 1998)
I Guardiani Del Cielo (*Tower of the Firstborn*; US: *The Sands of Time*) (Radiotelevisione Italiana, Italy, 1998)
The Mummy (Universal, USA, 1999)
Straight Shooter (Perathon Film und Fernsehproduktions GmbH/Senator Film, Germany, 1999)
Pø fremmed mark (*Foreign Fields*) (Balboa Enterprises ApS/Nordisk Film, Denmark, 1999)
Entre Chiens et Loups (*Between Dogs and Wolves*) (US: *Break of Dawn*) (Alexandre Films/Canal + France 2/Mediapro Pictures, France, 2002)
Les Oreilles Sur Le Dos (*Ears on the Back*) (FR3/Pierre Javaux Prod., French TV, 2002)
Vendredi Soir (*Friday Evening*) (Arena Films/France 2/Canal + France, 2002)
Ripoux 3 (*Crooked Cops 3* U.S. : *Part-Time Cops*) (Gaumont/CPZ Prod./Plaza Prod./TF1Films Prod./TPS Star/Sogecinema, France, 2003)
Secondhand Lions (New Line, USA, 2003)
Henry X (Golden Shadow Pictures, USA, 2003)
Les Gaous (*The Bumpkin*) (Comedie Star/Matrix/Studio Babelsberg Motion Pictures GmbH, France-Germany-UK, 2004)
Cause Toujours! (*Today's Cause!*) (Art-Light Prod., France, 2004)
Emmenez-moi (*Take Me Away with You*) (Vendredi Film, France, 2005)

THE SPANISH FOREIGN LEGION

It is necessary to give Spain its due, for that romantic land has also had a foreign legion since January 1920. Unlike their Gallic counterpart, native Spaniards were allowed to join and made up about 75% of the outfit. They first saw service in Morocco against the Riff, quickly establishing themselves as Spain's most elite force. They eventually allied themselves with the French Foreign Legion and defeated the Riff in 1926, bringing the seven-year Riff War to an end. They remained in Morocco and the Spanish Sahara until 1976, when they were withdrawn except for the cities of Ceuta and Melilla. In recent years they have acted as a peace-keeping force for NATO. Their strength in 1979 was estimated at 10,000 members. After they stopped accepting foreigners in 1987, the term "foreign" was dropped from their name. The following films featured that select corps.

In 1921, a series entitled *España en Africa* (*Spain in Africa*) was produced. It included two documentary films about the Spanish Foreign Legion: *Operaciones en Ras-Medua* and *Regimientos de Heroicos*.

POR LA PATRIA Y EL REY-- MEMORIAS DE UN LEGIONARIO
(FOR COUNTRY AND KING--MEMOIRS OF A LEGIONNAIRE)
Atlantida Films (Spain). Released 1923. Madrid premiere November 25, 1921. Director and Producer: Rafael Salvador. Cinematography: Vicente Guillo. Titles: Pedro de Repide.

Synopsis: A man enlists in the Spanish Legion during the Riff War in an attempt to forget a woman. There, he hopes to die a hero's death.

LOS HEROES DE LA LEGION
(HEROES OF THE LEGION)
Ediciones Lopez Rienda (Spain). Released April 30, 1928. Director: Rafael Lopez Rienda. Writer: Rafael L. Rienda, from his novel *Juan Leon, legionario.* Photography: Carlos Pahissa. Cast: Manuel Chavarri, Pablo Rossi, Carmen Sanchez, Ricardo Vargas, Ricardo Vayos.

Synopsis: Spanish legionnaires battle the Riff in the early stages of the Riff War, when Spain suffered several setbacks.

DER LEGIONAR
(THE LEGIONNAIRE)
Ideal Film Gmbh (Germany). Released July 3, 1929. 90mins. Director: Louis Ralph. Producers: Heinrich Nebenzahl, Gustav Schwab. Story: Louis Ralph. Screenplay: Curt Siodmak. Cinematography: Akos Farkas, Alex Graatkjaer. Art Direction: Edgar G. Ulmer. Production Mgr.: William Zeiske. Music: Werner Schmidt-Boelcke. Cast: Hans Stüwe, Eva von Berne, Alexander Murski, Harry Hardt, Eugen Burg, Henry Bender, Elsa Reval, Pedro Larranaga, Alexander Granach, Carl Walter Meyer, Louis Treumann, Ilse Gery, Elfriede Borodin, Charles Francois, Karl Falkenberg, Harry Pollandt, Hans Sanden. Alternate titles: *Flucht in Die Fremdenlegion* (*Flight into the Foreign Legion*); *Die Flucht Der Fremden Legionare* (*The Flight of the Foreign Legionnaire*).

This was begun as a French Foreign Legion film, but was so anti-French that the French government complained, and the setting was shifted to the Spanish Foreign Legion.

VORTRAG ZU DEM BILDSTREIFEN: DIE FLUCHT IN DIE FREMDENLEGION
(INTRODUCTION TO THE FILM: FLIGHT INTO THE FOREIGN LEGION)
Carl Wolf (Berlin). Released November 14, 1929. Documentary about the previous film.

LA BANDERA
(THE FLAG)
(AKA *LA GRANDE RELEVE*)
(U.S.: *ESCAPE FROM YESTERDAY*)
Societé Nouvelle de Cinematographie (France). Released May 2, 1935. 96mins. U.S. Distributor: Hoffberg Prods. Inc. (1939). Director: Julien Duvivier. Screenplay: J. Duvivier, Charles Spaak, from the novel by Pierre Dumarchais. Photography: Jules Kruger. Art Direction: Jacques Krauss. Editor: Marthe Poncin. Original Music: Roland Manuel, Jean Wiener. Assistant Directors: Jesus Castro Blanco, Robert Vernay. Producer: A. Gargour. Cast: Jean Gabin, Annabella, Robert Le Vigan, Raymond Ainos, Viviane Romance, Robert

Ozanne, Pierre Renoir, Gaston Modot, Margo Lion, Charles Granval, Reine Paulet, Jesus Castro Blanco, Maurice Lagrenée, Robert Ancelin, Louis Florencie, Little Jacky.

Synopsis: A Parisian named Pierre murders a man, and then flees to Barcelona in Spain. His wallet is stolen at a café. Lacking money and identification papers, he is unable to find work, so he joins the Spanish Foreign Legion. A fellow Frenchman joins at the same time and ingratiates himself with Pierre. After some time, Pierre learns from a newspaper item that there is a price of 50,000 francs on his head. He becomes suspicious of his friend. One day at a popular club, Pierre meets and falls in love with a Bedouin woman and marries her soon after. He makes plans with her to live elsewhere when his time in the Legion is up, but he must be sure about his friend. He asks his wife to play along with the man, who was interested in her but did not know she was Pierre's wife. She does and discovers the man is a cop after Pierre. When the Riff War breaks out, their captain asks for volunteers to hold a fort in the mountains whose previous garrison had been wiped out. No one steps forward until the captain informs them that he will be leading the group of twenty-four men; then everyone volunteers. The captain tells his lieutenant to select two dozen men. Among them are Pierre and the cop. At the rundown fort they are surrounded; any man who leaves the fort is shot immediately by the Riff. Soon only Pierre and the cop are left. Just as a relief force arrives, Pierre is fatally shot. The cop relays the sad news to Pierre's wife.

A short feature documentary on the making of this film is included on the 2007 European DVD release of the restored version. Directed by Jacques Viallon and produced by SND, it is from 1966 and entitled *Histoire de la Legion Etrangére*. In the Musée de la Legion Etrangére in Aubagne, France, a French Foreign Legion officer, Commandant de Bataillon Philippe Guyot, tells the story of the Legion, while pointing to various artifacts of the Museum. The movie is illustrated with excerpts from *La Bandera*, with Guyot explaining the similarities and differences (mainly spirit and mystique) between the French and the Spanish Legions.

L'UOMO DELLA LEGIONE
(MAN OF THE LEGION)

Continental Cine/Duro Films. Italy/Spain. Released March 1940 (Italy). June 1941 (Spain). 67mins. Director: Romolo Marcellini. Story: Gian Gaspare Napolitano. Screenplay: R. Marcellini, G. G. Napolitano. Cinematography: Mario Craveri. Editor: Vincenzo Zampi. Original Music: Mario Chiari. Set Decoration: G. Raimondi, Alberto Tavazzi. Production Design: G. Raimondi, Alberto Tavazzi. Asst. Director: Mario Chiari. Cast: Roberto Rey, Pastora Peña, Mario Ferrari, Juan de Landa, Carlo Ninchi, Corrado Racca, Giovanni Grasso, Maruja Muñoz, Carmen Navaquas, Emilio Petacci, Milly Senno, Jole Tinta, Liu Vega.

¡A MI LA LEGION!
TO ME THE LEGION!)
(aka *FOLLOW THE LEGION*)

Cifesa-UPCE-Hispania Artisfilms (Spain). Released May 11, 1942. 82mins. Director: Juan De Orduea. Photography: Alfredo Fraile. Story: Raul Cancio and Jaime Harcia. Herranz. Editor: Antonio Canovas. Art Direction: Emilio Ferrer. Music: Juan Quintero. Art Director: Emilio Ferrer. Sound: Enrique de la Riva. Cast: Alfredo Mayo, Luis Peña, Manuel Luna, Pilar

La Bandera (Societé Nouvelle de Cinematographie, 1935) Poster

Soler, Miguel Pozanco, Manuel Arbo, Rufino Ingles, Fortunato Bernal, Arturo Marin, Fred Galiana.

¡A Mi La Legion! (Cifesa-UPCE-Hispania-Artisfilms, 1942) Miguel Pozando, Luis Peña, Alfredo Mayo

Synopsis: A Legion veteran and a young recruit form a friendship during the final days of the Riff War. The younger man is actually a prince of a (fictional) European kingdom. Ten years later the older man visits that country at a time when the prince is in danger and prevents an attack upon him. The grateful prince makes him a councilor. After more time passes, the older man learns of an uprising in the Spanish Legion in Africa against the republican government. Both he and the prince return to the Legion.

LA LEGION

Hermic Films (Spain). Released 1948. 8mins. Director: Manuel H. Sanjuan. Writer: Santos Nuñez. Photography: Segismundo Perez de Pedro. Music: Fernando Carrascosa and Juan Alvarez Garcia. A documentary short about the Spanish Legion.

TRUHANES DE HONOR
(ROGUES OF HONOR)

Cooperativa del Cinema de Madrid (Spain). Released 1950. 91mins. Director: Eduardo Garcia Maroto. Story: Jaime Garcia. Screenplay: J. G. Herranz. Cinematography: Juan Mariné and Carlos Pahissa. Original Music: Jesus Garcia Leoz. Cast: Antonio Almoros,

Manuel Arbo, Francisco Bernal, José Bodalo, Teofilo Palou, Emma Penella, Gustavo Re, Emilio Santiago.

Synopsis: César and Carlos fight on a wharf; there is a gunshot and César falls into the water. Carlos flees and joins the Spanish Legion. Later, in Morocco, César turns up alive; he is also a legionnaire. Their animosity is renewed; Carlos winds up in a disciplinary battalion.

SABADO LEGIONARIO
(SATURDAY LEGIONNAIRE)

Centauro (Spain). Released 1988. Director: Javier Codesal Perez. Screenplay: J. C. Perez. Photography: José Luis Ureea. Editor: José Manuel Iriarte. Documentary short showing military and religious aspects of the Legion in traditional ceremonies.

Unrealized French Foreign Legion Projects:

The Bugle Sounds (M-G-M, USA) Canceled due to the death of its star, Lon Chaney.
Par Le Sang Verse (*Because of the Blood Shed*) (France)
Le Hommes Sans Passe (*Men Without a Past*) (France)
Man Stands Alone (M-G-M, USA)

Television versions of *Beau Sabreur*, *Beau Ideal* and *Wages of Virtue* for the BBC were canceled due to the death of Douglas Camfield, who had produced the 1982 BBC version of *Beau Geste*.

§

Truhanes de Honor (Cooperativa del Cinema de Madrid, 1950) Poster

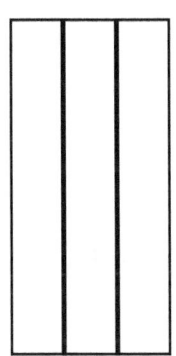

Bibliography

Baxter, John. *The Cinema of Josef von Sternberg*. London: A. Zwemmer, 1971. New York: A.S. Barnes, 1971.

Bigland, Eileen. *Ouida, The Passionate Victorian*. London: Jarrolds Ltd., 1950.

Braff, Richard E. *The Universal Silents*. Jefferson, NC: McFarland & Co., 1999.

Colman, Juliet B. *Ronald Colman: A Very Private Person*. New York: William Morrow & Co., 1975.

Dickens, Homer. *The Films of Marlene Dietrich*. Secaucus, NJ: Citadel Press, 1968.

Edmonds, I. G. *Big U--Universal in the Silent Days*. South Brunswick & New York: A.S. Barnes & Co., 1977.

Everson, William K. *The Films of Laurel and Hardy*. Secaucus, NJ: Citadel Press, 1967.

Gifford, Denis. *The British Film Catalogue, 1895-1985*. New York: Facts on File, 1986.

Green, Roger L. *A. E. W. Mason*. London: Parrish, 1952.

Guinle, Pierre & Ricci, Guiseppe. *Filmografia della Legione Straniera*. Rimini, Italy: Riminicinema, 1992.

Jelst-Blanc, Jean-Jacques. *Biblio Fernandel*. Paris: Editions Alain Le Feuvre, 1981.

Lenburg, Jeff, Maurer, Joan Howard & Lenburg, Greg. *The Three Stooges Scrapbook* . Secaucus, NJ: Citadel Press, 1982.

Louvish, Simon. *Stan and Ollie: The Roots of Comedy*. New York: Thomas Dunne Books, St. Martin's Press, 2002.

Lubow, Arthur. *The Reporter Who Would Be King--A Biography of Richard Harding Davis*. New York: Scribner's, 1992.

Mason, A.E.W. *The Winding Stair*. New York: Grosset & Dunlap, 1925.

Munden, Kenneth W. Executive Editor. *The American Film Institute Catalog--Feature Films, 1921-1930*. New York and London: R. R. Bowker Co., 1971.

Okuda, Ted. *The Monogram Checklist*. Jefferson, NC: McFarland, 1987.

O'Leary, Liam. *Rex Ingram--Master of the Silent Cinema*. Dublin: Academy Press, 1980.

Ouida. *Under Two Flags*. Philadelphia: J. B. Lippincott, 1901.

Porch, Douglas. *The French Foreign Legion*. New York: HarperCollins, 1991.

Quirk, Lawrence J. *The Films of Ronald Colman*. Secaucus, NJ: Citadel Press, 1977.

Shaheen, Jack G. *Reel Bad Arabs*. Olive New York: Branch Press, 2001.

Skal, David J. & Savada, Elias. *Dark Carnival*. New York: Anchor Books, 1995.

Slide, Anthony. *Frank Lloyd--Master of Screen Melodrama*. Albany, GA: BearManor Media, 2009

Smith, R. Dixon. *Ronald Colman, Gentleman of the Cinema*. Jefferson, NC: McFarland, 1991

Spoto, Donald. *Laurence Olivier, A Biography*. New York: HarperCollins, 1992.

Stone, Rob. *Laurel or Hardy*. Temecula, CA: Split Reel Books, 1996.

Taves, Brian. *Robert Florey*. Metuchen, NJ: Scarecrow Press, 1987.

Taves, Brian. *The Romance of Adventure*. Jackson, MI: University Press of Mississippi, 1993.

Terrace, Vincent. Encyclopedia of TV Series, Pilots and Specials 1937-1973. New York: Zoetrope, 1986.

Bibliography

Thompson, Frank T. *William Wellman.* Metuchen, NJ: Scarecrow Press, 1983.

Thompson, Frank T. *Lost Films--Important Movies that Disappeared.* New York & Toronto. Citadel Press, 1996.

Tuska, Jon. *The Vanishing Legion.* Jefferson, NC & London: McFarland & Co., 1989.

Vardac, Nicholas A. *Stage to Screen.* Cambridge, MA: Harvard University Press, 1949.

Wellard, James. *The French Foreign Legion.* Boston & Toronto: Little, Brown & Co., 1974.

Wren, P. C. *Beau Geste.* New York: Grosset & Dunlap, 1926.

Wren, P. C. *Beau Sabreur.* New York: Frederick A. Stokes, 1926.

Wren, P. C. *Beau Ideal.* New York: Grosset & Dunlap, 1928.

Wylie, I. A. R. *The Foreign Legion* (Photoplay Edition of *The Red Mirage*). New York: Grosset & Dunlap, 1928.

ARTICLES

Eyles, Allan. "The State of the Legion" *Focus on Film.* October 1977.

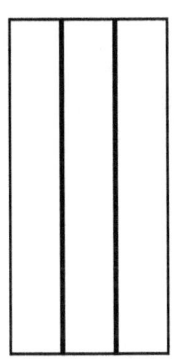

Index

A

Abbott and Costello –121, 122

B

Bara, Theda – 2, 3

Beau Geste (book) – 17, 23

Beau Geste (1926) – 4, 17, 18, 19, 20

Beau Geste (1939) – 20, 21, 31, 32

Beau Geste (1966) – 21, 22

Beau Ideal (book) - 23

Beau Ideal (1931) - 23, 24

Beau Sabreur (book) - 23

Beau Sabreur (1928) – 23, 24

Brabin, Charles – 3

Brenon, Herbert – 17, 19, 24

Brent, Evelyn – 23

Browning, Tod – 3, 4

Buckner, Robert - 77

C

Capt. Macklin (1915) – 37

Carradine, John – 5

Chasseurs D'Afrique – 1. 2. 3. 149

Cigarette, or Under Two Flags – 131

Colbert, Claudette – 4, 13

Colman, Ronald – 4, 5, 14, 17, 19

Connolly, Robert – 67

Covered Wagon, The (1923) – 23

Cruze, James – 23

D

Davis, Richard Harding – 37

Dean, Priscilla – 3

de la Ramee, Marie Louise (see "Ouida")

Desert Song, The (play) - 67

Desert Song, The (1929) – 71

Desert Song, The (1944) – 72

Desert Song, The (1953) – 72

Donlevy, Brian – 32, 33

Dreier, Hans – 32

F

Florey, Robert – 72, 77

Forbes, Ralph – 24

Four Feathers, The (book) – 37

G

Gem (film company) – 2

Gish, Lillian – 24

Goldwyn, Samuel – 17

H

Hamilton, Neil – 19

Hammerstein, Oscar H. – 67

Harbach, Otto – 67

Hayward, Susan – 32

Hurley, Arthur – 67

K

Kerry, Norman – 37

L

Laurel and Hardy – 113, 120

Lloyd, Frank – 5, 13, 14

Lost Horizon (1937) – 4

M

Mademoiselle Modiste – 67

Mandel, Frank – 67

Mason, A. E. W. – 37

McLaglen, Victor – 5

Mutiny on the Bounty (1935) – 4

N

Nolan, Mary – 37

O

Odell, Robert – 32

Old Ironsides (1926) – 23

Ouida (Marie Louise de la Ramee) – 1, 2, 5

P

Prisoner of Zenda, The (1937) – 4

INDEX

R

Ralston, Esther – 23

Red Mirage, The (book) – 37

Riff War – 151

Romberg, Sigmund – 67

S

Savalas, Telly – 21

Simon, Simone – 4, 13

Sloman, Edward – 37

Smith and Dale – 113

Soldiers of Fortune (book) – 37

Spanish Foreign Legion – 151

Stone, Lewis – 37

Swanson, Gloria – 24

T

Tale of Two Cities, A (1935) – 4

Tellegen, Lou – 37

Thackery, Bud – 21

Thompson, Woodman – 67

Three Stooges, The – 113

Trail of the Lonesome Pine, The (1936) – 32

U

Under Two Flags (book) – 1, 2

Under Two Flags (Gem, 1912) – 2

Under Two Flags (Thanhouser, 1912) – 2

Under Two Flags (1915) – 2

Under Two Flags (1916) – 2, 3

Under Two Flags (1922) – 3

Under Two Flags (1936) – 4, 5, 13, 14

Under Two Jags (play) – 131

Under Two Jags (1923) – 113, 131

Unknown, The (1915) – 37

V

Vail, Lester – 29

W

Waters, John – 23

Wellman, William – 20, 23

Winding Stair, The (1925) – 37

Wings (1927) – 23

Wren, P(erciva) C(hristopher) – 17

Y

Young, Loretta – 29

Z

Zanuck, Darryl F. – 14

Zukor, Adolph – 17

www.ingramcontent.com/pod-product-compliance
Lightning Source LLC
Chambersburg PA
CBHW051933160426
43198CB00012B/2134